SCM PAPERBACKS
by William Barclay

THE MIND OF JESUS

CRUCIFIED AND CROWNED

NEW TESTAMENT WORDS

THE MASTER'S MEN

PRAYERS FOR THE CHRISTIAN YEAR

EPILOGUES AND PRAYERS

LETTERS TO THE SEVEN CHURCHES

THE LORD'S SUPPER

WILLIAM BARCLAY

The Mind of Jesus

SCM PRESS LTD
BLOOMSBURY STREET LONDON

334 01014 4

First published 1960
Second impression 1963
Third impression 1965
Fourth impression 1968
Fifth impression 1971
Sixth impression 1973
Seventh impression 1975
Eighth impression 1976

© *SCM Press Ltd 1960*

Printed in Great Britain by
Fletcher & Son Ltd, Norwich

CONTENTS

To the Students of
Trinity College, Glasgow
Past and Present

PREFACE

THE chapters of this book originally appeared as a series of weekly articles in the pages of the *British Weekly*, and I am very grateful to its editor, the Rev. Dennis Duncan, for giving me permission to republish them. The material has been extensively rewritten and refashioned, so that indeed in many parts of the book it bears but little relation to its original form.

The aim of this book is to try to make it possible to understand the mind of Jesus a little better. The material on which it is based is the material of the first three Gospels; it does not use the Fourth Gospel, nor does it use the Epistles, for the study of that material is another task in itself. It is my conviction that in the first three Gospels we have a reliable account of the ministry and of the teaching of Jesus. I know very well that it is quite true that we do not possess the materials to write a biography of Jesus, but at the same time I am convinced, and the more I study them the more I am convinced, that we have in these Gospels material on which we can rely to reconstruct the basic events of Jesus' life, to understand his teaching, and at least to some extent to enter into his mind.

In this book I have not wished to argue; I have simply wished to set down the picture of Jesus as I see it and to set out what he means to me. I am well aware that there are those who will differ from the point of view of this book even to the point of violence, but I can only say to them that in the Jesus of this book I have found him who is Saviour of men and my Saviour. I do not think that there is anything new in this book; its debts are too many and too obvious to detail. Throughout it my one aim has been to try to make the figure of Jesus more vividly alive, so that we may know him better and love him more.

This book stops at the Transfiguration. It is the first book of a trilogy (to be completed in 1961). The story of Jesus is continued in *Crucified and Crowned*. Other material will be found in *Jesus as They Saw Him*.

One word more—I cannot allow this book to go out without

expressing my very sincere gratitude to Rev. David L. Edwards, the Editor of the SCM Press, for all his help. In the preparation of this book he has gone far beyond the normal duties of an editor, and his counsel, his advice, and his guidance, and, not infrequently, his criticism have saved me from errors of fact, and even more from errors of judgment. He is, of course, not responsible for anything that I have written, but his continual help has done a very great deal to give this book any value that it has.

WILLIAM BARCLAY

Trinity College,
Glasgow

ACKNOWLEDGEMENTS

The cover: the illustration is of Epstein's *Majestas* in Llandaff Cathedral, reproduced by permission of the Dean.

The lines by William Soutar are from 'The Carpenter', in *Collected Poems*, Andrew Dakers Ltd. 1948, p. 38.

The lines by James Weldon Johnson are from 'The Creation', in *God's Trombones, Some Negro Sermons in Verse*, George Allen and Unwin, 1929, pp. 23 ff.

1

THE GREAT DISCOVERY

IT may be said that there are two great beginnings in the life of every man who has left his mark upon history. There is the day when he is born into the world; and there is the day when he discovers why he was born into the world. There was a day in the life of Jesus when he made that great discovery.

The greatest festival of the Jews was the festival of the Passover. On that day the Jews have always remembered, and still remember, how the hand of God delivered them from their bondage in the land of Egypt. It fell on 15th Nisan, in the middle of April, and it was kept in Jerusalem. It was one of the three obligatory festivals—the others were Pentecost and Tabernacles—to which every adult male Jew who lived within fifteen miles of Jerusalem was bound by the law to come. But such was the sanctity of this festival that Jews from all over the world gathered in Jerusalem to celebrate it, and a Jew of the Dispersion would save for a lifetime to keep one Passover in the Holy City.

The most careful preparations were made for the Passover. The roads were levelled and the bridges were repaired; the wayside tombs were whitewashed, lest any traveller should accidentally touch one of them, and, because of his contact with a dead body, become unclean (Num. 19.11). For six weeks before the festival it was the story and the meaning of the Passover which formed the subject of teaching in every school and of preaching in every synagogue. No one in Palestine could be unaware that the Passover was near. To any seriously-minded boy, to any boy with a sense of history and of country and an awareness of God, the day when he attended his first Passover in Jerusalem was bound to be a day of days.

So the day came when the boy Jesus was to attend his first Passover festival in Jerusalem (Luke 2.41-52). Everything on the roads, in the school, in the synagogue had for weeks been saying: 'The Passover is at hand!' And now the time had come.

It is the better part of a hundred miles from Nazareth to Jerusalem. It would take a week for the slow caravan to make its

long journey. All the time of the journey Jesus was thinking of
the Passover, and of how God had once delivered his people,
and with every step of the way his expectation was kindled to
a brighter flame.

A city that is set on a hill cannot be hid, and the astonishing
sight of Jerusalem appeared to Jesus' eyes. Josephus describes
the wonder of the Temple. 'The outward face of the Temple in
its front wanted nothing that was likely to surprise either men's
minds or their eyes; for it was covered all over with plates of
gold of great weight, and, at the first rising of the sun, reflected
back a very fiery splendour, and made those who forced themselves to look upon it to turn away their eyes, just as they would
have done at the sun's own rays. The Temple appeared to stran-
gers, when they were at a distance, like a mountain covered with
snow, for those parts of it that were not gilt were exceeding
white.'[1] There was a thrill in the mind of the boy Jesus as he
saw the gleaming Temple ahead, and as he climbed Mount Sion
with the Passover pilgrims, singing, as generations of pilgrims
had sung: 'I was glad when they said to me, Let us go to the
house of the Lord' (Ps. 122.1). He was sure that the Passover
was going to give him the greatest experience in his life—and
it did, although not in the way that he had expected it. So Jesus
came to Jerusalem with expectation in his heart, and something
happened.

On the afternoon of the day in the evening of which the Passover was observed the Passover lambs were killed. The lamb was
not simply the main dish at the Passover meal; the lamb was a
sacrifice; and, therefore, the lamb had to be slain in the Temple
courts. There was one part of every slain beast which belonged
to God, the blood. The Jews identified the blood of a living
creature with the life of the creature. It was a natural identification, for as the blood flows away the life flows away. To God
alone life belongs, and, therefore, to God alone the blood of
every slain creature belongs, and it must be offered to him. So
Joseph with Jesus took the lamb to the Temple to be slain so that
the blood might be offered to God.

The *Mishnah,* the codified law of the Jews, describes the

[1]   Josephus, *Wars of the Jews* 5.5.6, Whiston's translation.

regulations for the killing of the lamb and the offering of the blood. 'The priests stood in rows, and in their hands were basons of silver and gold. In one row all the basons were of silver and in another row all the basons were of gold. They were not mixed up together. Nor had the basons bases, lest the priests should set them down and the blood congeal. An Israelite slaughtered his own offering, and the priest caught the blood. The priest passed the bason to his fellow, and he to his fellow, each receiving a full bason and giving back an empty one. The priest nearest to the Altar tossed the blood in one action against the base of the Altar.'[1]

Let us think what this means. On one occasion in the reign of Nero the governor Cestius took a census of the number of lambs slain, in order to show Nero how many Jews attended the Passover festival. The number slain was 256,500.[2] Even if the figure be an exaggeration, as so many ancient figures are, the number must certainly have been immense.

Let us try to visualize the scene in the Temple courts on the afternoon before the evening of the Passover meal. The hundreds of thousands of worshippers, each one of them slitting the throat of the lamb and allowing the blood to drain away, the long line of the priests leading to the altar, the bowls of blood being passed from hand to hand finally to be dashed against the base of the altar, the odour and the reek of blood, the marble pavements of the Temple slippery with the blood of the lambs, the atmosphere of a vast slaughter house and butcher's shop—that is what Jesus saw. And in the mind of the young Jesus there arose the beginning of a great disillusionment. The Passover festival was intended to bring men closer to God. How could this welter of blood do that? Already, young as he was, Jesus knew God as his Father, and in Jerusalem at the Passover festival, he had expected to encounter God as never before—and now this. The expectation was turned to bewilderment; and the expected thrill became the unexpected disillusionment. In all this welter of blood there was no God for a wounded conscience, a contrite spirit and a seeking mind.

[1] *Mishnah,* Pesahim 5.5f., Danby's translation.
[2] Josephus, *Wars of the Jews* 6.9.3.

But to Jesus there was left still another hope. The supreme court of the Jews, embodying the highest wisdom of the nation, was the Sanhedrin with its seventy members, presided over by the High Priest. Normally the Sanhedrin met in private in its own Hall of Hewn Stone, and there it discussed the matters of the law. But during the Passover time the Sanhedrin met in public, and any who wished might listen to the discussions of the learned men. Already Jesus was steeped in the prophets; Hosea and Isaiah were his familiar friends. Already he moved familiarly amidst the laws of Deuteronomy. Now he would go and hear the wisdom of the wise, and, even if the priestly ritual had been a grim disillusionment, surely here he would find the closer contact with God for which he was seeking. And once again bewilderment came to him. It was not of justice and mercy, love and holiness that they were talking. They were talking of the Sabbath law. The Sabbath law forbade work on the Sabbath day. To carry a burden was to work. Yes, but what constituted a burden? Could, or could not, a man go out on the Sabbath with nails in his shoes or sandals? Could, or could not, a man wear a false tooth on the Sabbath? If a cripple went out with a wooden leg was he carrying a burden? A man might not lift and carry and throw a stone on the Sabbath day. But did that apply to a stone big enough to fling at a bird, or big enough to throw at cattle? A man might not write on the Sabbath day; but did that apply, if he wrote in some fluid which left no permanent mark? These are all questions which are actually discussed in the *Mishnah* (Shabbath 6.2-5,8; 8.4-6). So they discussed the minutiae of the law, the legalistic details which for the scribes and Pharisees constituted religion. And there was no way to God there, no way to heal a broken heart, no way to assure a man of forgiveness for his sins, no way to make a man feel certain that God is his Father in heaven.

Jesus had come to Jerusalem with the most eager hopes and expectations. His heart had thrilled when he saw the Holy City gleaming in the distance. He had looked forward to the Passover festival with all his heart. And he had discovered that the way of the priests was completely unavailing. What had this butchery of lambs to do with bringing a man nearer to God, and what had this welter of blood to say about the God whose name is

Father? He had discovered that the way of the wise men was unavailing. What had these petty legalistic details to do with justice and mercy and love? What had these arid discussions about the Sabbath law to do with a man who had known the tears of things, and who was bitterly conscious that he was soiled with sin? He had suddenly discovered that the whole paraphernalia of sacrifice was a vast irrelevance, and the whole apparatus of the law a barrier to God.

Somewhere Jewish religion had gone wrong, and had lost the way. Sacrifice had meant the giving of one's best to God, and what is one's best but oneself? But sacrifice had become a ritual slaughter of beasts instead of a self-dedication to God. The law had been meant to be a thing in which a man might find his delight, the basis of a life lived in reverence to God and in respect for men and for human personality, and instead it had become an unending collection of petty rules and regulations. It was not so much that Jesus felt the need to break with Jewish religion; it was rather that he felt the need to rediscover Jewish religion. It was not that he wished to destroy Jewish religion; he wished rather to fulfil it, and to rescue it from the shallows and the byways in which it had got lost.

And then out of the disillusionment there came to Jesus the voice and the revelation of God. There came the voice of the God whom he knew, as none other had ever known, as his Father. And God was saying: 'The priests have lost me; the wise men have lost me; the people seek me, and cannot find me. *It is your task to tell men of me and to bring them to my love.*'

On that day in the Temple Jesus had a unique experience of God as his Father; and he had a unique realization that it was his life's work to bring men to God and to bring God to men, in a way that neither priest nor rabbi could ever do. It was to be many a long year before he could set out on his task, but from that day his task was clear to him. He knew why he had come into the world.

2

WAITING FOR THE CALL

Even when a man discovers the task for which God has sent him into the world, he has still another problem to solve, the problem of when to begin upon it. If he begins too soon, he will begin without the necessary preparation and equipment for the task. If he waits until too late, he may never begin at all. If he chooses the wrong moment, his work may be foredoomed to failure even before he begins.

In the Temple Jesus had realized the futility of human ways of seeking for God, and he had made the great discovery that he had been sent into the world to bring all men to God; and now he had to await the call from God to set out upon his work. And Jesus waited long. He was twelve when the revelation in the Temple came to him (Luke 2.42); he was thirty when he left Nazareth to begin upon his work (Luke 3.23). Eighteen years is a long time to wait; but the silent years were not the wasted years, for they were years of preparation for the task that no one else in the world could do. Throughout the years Jesus was learning all the time.

He was learning the basic knowledge and the basic skills which are every man's equipment for life. As Luke tells us, he increased in wisdom and in stature (Luke 2.52). He learned to read, for we know that the day was to come when he was to read the lesson from the prophets in the synagogue in Nazareth (Luke 4.16). He learned to write, which in those days was a much rarer accomplishment. In the story of the woman taken in adultery, we are told that Jesus stooped down and wrote on the ground (John 8.8). In that passage an Armenian manuscript dating to AD 989 makes the curious addition that it was the sins of the woman's accusers which Jesus wrote on the ground, and that is why they slipped silently away. 'He himself, bowing his head, was writing with his finger on the earth, to declare their sins; and they were seeing their several sins on the stones.' Jesus was learning the skills which every boy must learn. There was a village school in Nazareth; to that village school Jesus must have gone. In that village school there was a nameless village schoolmaster, whose name no man will ever know, and yet that schoolmaster taught the Son of God. Many a teacher is doing a work far greater than he knows.

He was learning to do a good day's work, for it was as the carpenter of Nazareth that men knew him (Mark 6.3). Jesus was the good craftsman. Justin Martyr tells us: 'He was in the habit of working as a carpenter when he was among men, making ploughs and yokes',[1] and there is a legend that Jesus of Nazareth made the best ox-yokes in all Galilee, and that men came from far and near to buy the yokes that Jesus made. Then as now craftsmen hung their trade sign and their slogan above their shops. Once Jesus said: 'My yoke is easy' (Matt. 11.30). The Greek word for *easy* is *chrēstos*, which means *well-fitting*, and some one has imagined that the sign above the door of the carpenter's shop in Nazareth was an ox-yoke with the words painted on it: 'My yokes fit well.'

It is, indeed, significant to note what the New Testament actually calls Jesus; it calls him a *tektōn* (Mark 6.3). A *tektōn* was more than a carpenter; he was a craftsman who could build a wall or a house, construct a boat, or make a table or a chair, or throw a bridge across a little stream. In the old days—and even now in the country places—there were men who, with the minimum of technical equipment and the maximum of the craftsman's inborn skill, could turn their hands to any job. In their hands wood and metal and stones become obedient, and such was Jesus. William Soutar, the Scots poet, wrote a poem about the craftsman's hands of Jesus:

> Glaidly he dressed the rochest deal
> To mak a kist or door;
> Strauchtly he drave the langest nail
> Wi' little sturt or stour.

> Monie a man as he gaed by,
> And monie a kintra wench,
> Wad watch the strang and souple hands
> That wrocht abune the bench.

[1] *Dialogue with Trypho* 88.

And aye sae true, sae tenderly,
Sae trysted wud they move
As they had been a lover's hands
That blindly kent their love.

In Nazareth Jesus got to himself the craftsman's strong and gentle hands.

He was winning the physical manhood to enable him to do his task. The time was to come when Jesus was to walk the roads of Palestine, and when he was to tell a would-be follower that the foxes had their holes and the birds of the air their nests, but that he had nowhere to lay his head (Luke 9.58). Jesus could never have lived the life he did live had he not been physically equipped for it. In those days a carpenter did not buy his wood from the saw-mill or from the wholesaler. He went out to the hill-side, chose his young tree, swung his axe, cut it down and carried it home on his shoulder. Certainly Jesus was no weak and anaemic person; he must have been bronzed and weather-beaten, in the perfection of physical manhood.

One of the great gaps in our knowledge of Jesus is that we do not know what in physical appearance he was like. In regard to this, tradition was divided into two. One line of thought began with Isaiah's picture of the Suffering Servant. 'His appearance was so marred, beyond human semblance' (Isa. 52.14). 'He had no form nor comeliness that we should look at him, and no beauty that we should desire him' (Isa. 53.2). Arguing from this, Irenaeus said that Jesus was weak, inglorious and without grace.[1] Origen said he was small, ill-favoured, and insignificant.[2] Cyril of Alexandria even went the length of saying that he was 'the ugliest of the children of men'. The other line of thought stemmed from Ps. 45.2: 'You are the fairest of the sons of men.' This line of thought painted Jesus in words and in pictures in the beauty of the Olympian gods.

The most famous of all descriptions is in the *Letter of Lentulus,* who purports to be governor of Jerusalem:

There has appeared here in our time, and still lives here, a man of great power named Jesus Christ. The people call him

[1]   *Against Heresies* 4.33.12.
[2]   *Against Celsus* 6.75.

a prophet of truth, and his disciples the Son of God. He raises the dead and cures the sick. He is in stature a man of middle height and well proportioned. He has a venerable face, of a sort to arouse both fear and love in those who see him. His hair is the colour of ripe chestnuts, smooth almost to the ears, but above them waving and curling, with a slightly bluish radiance, and it flows over his shoulders. It is parted in the middle on the top of his head, after the fashion of the people of Nazareth. His brow is smooth and very calm, with a face without wrinkle or blemish, lightly tinged with red. His nose and mouth are faultless. His beard is luxuriant and unclipped, of the same colour as his hair, not long but parted at the chin. His eyes are expressive and brilliant. He is terrible in reproof, sweet and gentle in admonition, cheerful without ceasing to be grave. He has never been seen to laugh, but often to weep. His figure is slender and erect; his hands and arms are beautiful to see. His conversation is serious, sparing and modest. He is the fairest of the children of men.

There are those who go the length of believing that this is nothing less than the police description of Jesus at the time of his arrest. But it is quite certain that the *Letter of Lentulus* is a forgery, although even then it is not impossible that it does embody a genuine tradition. It may be that we have to say of the appearance of Jesus, with Augustine, 'We are utterly ignorant.'[1] But this we can say, that in the silent years in Nazareth Jesus was building up the physical manhood without which he could not have faced or completed his task.

Throughout the silent years Jesus was learning the meaning of family life. The name for God which came most naturally to the lips of Jesus was Father; and the very use of that word is itself a very beautiful compliment to Joseph. It was said of Martin Luther that he hesitated to pray the Lord's Prayer and to say 'Our Father', because his own father had been so stern, so unbending, so unsympathetic that the word 'father' was not a word which he loved. To Jesus the name 'father' was the most natural and the most precious name for God, and it was in the home at Nazareth that he must have learned the meaning of that word.

[1] *Concerning the Trinity* 8.4f.

There were words which Jesus heard in the home in Nazareth which lingered in his mind all his days. Once he came to a little girl whom all others thought to be dead, and said softly: *'Talitha, cumi'*, which means, as we might say, 'Little lamb, get up!' (Mark 5.41). Where did Jesus hear a child called 'Little lamb'? Surely these were the words which he had heard the gentle Mary croon over himself and over his brothers and sisters, when they were very young. Throughout the years Jesus was discovering that it was God indeed who had set the solitary in families (Ps. 68.6). He was no monkish ascetic; he grew up within a home.

The work in the shop and the life in the family were both parts of the essential education and preparation of Jesus for his task, for through them his full identity with men was established. In the shop he knew the problem and the anxiety of making a living for a household. He knew the problem of dealing with unreasonable people. He learned to see men at their best and at their worst and as they were. In the home he had to solve the universal problem of living together. Jesus did not live a secluded, isolated, protected life, on which the wind was not allowed to blow. He knew the life of the men whom he had come to save.

Throughout the silent years Jesus learned to love God's world, and to see God in creation and in common things. Jesus grew to manhood in the loveliest part of Palestine. Around the Sea of Galilee there was the Plain of Gennesareth, and the Jews sometimes said that the word Gennesareth meant Prince of Gardens. They called that plain 'the unequalled garden of God'. They called the countryside around Sepphoris 'a land flowing with milk and honey'. There was a Jewish proverbial saying that it was easier to raise a legion of olive trees in Galilee than to bring up one child in the rest of Palestine. Merrill in his book on Galilee lists the trees which grew there in the time of Jesus— the vine, the olive, the fig, the oak, the walnut, the terebinth, the palm, the cedar, the cypress, the balsam, the fir-tree, the pine, the sycomore, the bay-tree, the myrtle, the almond, the pomegranate, the citron, the oleander. In Galilee, said Josephus, trees which would not grow together elsewhere grew in the same place, as if nature were doing violence to herself.[1]

[1]   *Wars of the Jews* 3.10.8.

It was in this land of loveliness that Jesus grew up. He learned to love the sight of the sower sowing his seed (Matt. 13.1-8); of the corn field ripening steadily under God's sun (Mark 4.26-29); of the mustard bush with the birds clustering round to steal the little black seeds (Mark 4.30-32); of the scarlet poppies and anemones blooming their one day on the hillside in raiment such as Solomon in his glory never wore (Matt. 6.28,29). Throughout the years Jesus was learning to look on the world as 'the garment of the living God'.

He was learning to use the common actions and happenings of life as windows through which to catch a glimpse of the truth and the glory of God. He watched his mother Mary using the leaven when she baked the bread (Matt. 13.33). He marked the frenzied search when a woman lost a silver coin amidst the rushes on the cottage floor (Luke 15.8f.). He knew what happened when some one carelessly put new wine into old bottles whose skins had lost their elasticity, and how a new patch on an old garment could leave things worse than ever (Matt. 9.16f.). He knew the joy of a village wedding feast (Matt. 9.15); he watched the fishermen with their nets (Matt. 13.47); he was moved by the care of the shepherd for his sheep (Luke 15.4-6). He watched the children playing at weddings and funerals in the village street (Matt. 11.16f.).

Few great teachers have had their feet so firmly planted on the ground as Jesus had. In these early years he was learning every day how to get from 'the here and now' to 'the there and then'. He was learning how near eternity is to time, and how to see God in the life and the actions and the things of every day.

Throughout the silent years Jesus was learning to dream. Nazareth itself is tucked away in a hollow of the hills, a secluded little town. But the extraordinary thing about Nazareth was that the world passed almost by its door. It has been said that Judaea was on the way to nowhere and Galilee was on the way to every-where, for the great roads of the East passed through Galilee. Jesus had only to climb the hilltop above the cup-like hollow of Nazareth and the passing world was at his feet. From there he could look down on the great Road of the Sea, the road which went from Damascus to Egypt, one of the greatest highways in the world with its merchantmen and its caravans. From there he could see the strategic Road of the East which went out from the Mediterranean coast to Parthia and to the eastern bounds of the Roman Empire with its Arab traders and its Roman legions clanking on their way. From there, if he looked westwards, he could see the blue waters of the Mediterranean, with the sails of the ships and the cargoes of those who do business in great waters.

So Jesus could climb the hilltop behind Nazareth, and from there he could see the roads coming and going to the ends of the earth. It was there that he must have dreamed his dreams, and it may be that it was there that something first said to him: 'I, when I am lifted up from the earth, will draw all men to myself' (John 12.32).

It was in the silent years that Jesus learned to pray. When he went out upon his task, it was his custom to take everything to God; again and again he withdrew from men to be alone with God. When he was in his last agony on the Cross, he prayed: 'Father, into thy hands I commit my spirit' (Luke 23.46). That is a quotation from Ps. 31.5 with the one word 'Father' added. But more, that was the first prayer which every Jewish mother taught her child to say, when he lay down to sleep at night, before the dark came down. It was with a prayer that he had learned at Nazareth on his lips that Jesus ended his agony and finished his task.

One thing more is to be added. Eighteen years is a long time to wait, and it may be that there was a very special reason for that delay. After the story of the birth of Jesus Joseph vanishes from the narrative. Even as early as the marriage feast at Cana of Galilee there is no word of Joseph being there (John 2.1-11). By far the most likely explanation is that Joseph was dead, and that the young Jesus had to take upon his shoulders the family business and the support of his mother Mary and of his younger brothers and sisters (Mark 6.3), and that he had to stay in Nazareth until there was some one in the family old enough to take over the carpenter's shop and to earn a living for the family. The day was to come when Jesus was to tell a story about a servant who because he had been faithful in a few things was made master over many things (Matt. 25.21-23). In that story Jesus was telling his own story, for it is quite certain that, if Jesus had not been faithful in the simple and the elementary duties of the home, God could never have given him the task of being the Saviour of the world. Throughout the silent years Jesus was learning many things; and in the performance of the simple duties he was proving himself for the task which God was to give him to do.

Let no man despise the simple duties of the home and the tasks which lie to his hand, for therein, for him as for Jesus, there is the purpose of God. Rabindranath Tagore, the Indian mystic, has a poem:

> At midnight the would-be ascetic announced: 'This is the time to give up my home and seek for God. Ah, who has held me so long in delusion here?' God whispered, 'I', but the ears of the man were stopped. With a baby asleep at her breast lay his wife, peacefully sleeping on one side of the bed. The man said: 'Who are ye that have fooled me so long?' The voice said again: 'They are God,' but he heard it not. The baby cried out in his dream, nestling closer to his mother. God commanded: 'Stop, fool; leave not thy home,' but he heard not. God sighed and complained: 'Why does my servant wander to seek me, forsaking me?'

The Son of God, when he came into this world, prepared himself to save the world by serving in a home.

3

THE HOUR STRIKES

THROUGHOUT the years of preparation Jesus was waiting for the sign which was to tell him that he must go out to begin the work for which he had come into the world. It was when he was thirty years of age (Luke 3.23) that the sign came and the hour unmistakably struck.

It was then that John the Baptizer burst upon the scene in Palestine. John was related to Jesus, for he was the son of Elisabeth, the kinswoman of Mary (Luke 1.36). He had been born to Zacharias, the priest, and to Elisabeth in the days of their old age, when all hope and expectation of a child had gone (Luke 1.5-25, 57-80). It was clear to his parents that John was no ordinary child, and that he had been sent into the world for no ordinary task, and it was in the solitudes of the desert and in the lonely places that John grew to manhood (Luke 1.80).

John appears on the scene, as it were, full grown. We know of his birth; we know of his sojourn in the desert; we know that he emerges as the baptizer of crowds of people in the River Jordan; but what training he had, where he found his message, and whence he took his rite of baptism we do not know. Although we have no certain knowledge, can we deduce anything about the origins of the message and the baptism of John? Let us begin by examining the possible sources of John's rite of baptism.

The pagan world was well acquainted with baptism. Baptism was the gateway through which the initiate entered many of the mystery religions. It was through baptism, as Tertullian notes, that the initiate entered into the worship of Isis, Mithra and the famous Eleusinian mysteries.[1] Clement of Alexandria tells us that lustrations, that is, washings, 'held the premier place' in the mystery ceremonies.[2] The worshipper of Dionysos experienced 'the pure washing', as Livy calls it.[3] When Apuleius tells of his

[1] *Concerning Baptism* 5.
[2] *Stromateis* 5.11.
[3] *Livy* 39.9.

own initiation, he tells that the officiating priest brought him to the baths, and, demanding pardon of the gods, washed him and purified his body, according to the custom.[1] Quite certainly the pagan world was familiar with baptism as an entry to the mystery religions in which the worshippers sought to find God. But it is very unlikely that John knew anything about these things, although there must have been at least some amongst those who came to him who knew, or had heard, about such baptisms.

The Jewish world knew about baptism, for the three necessary elements through which a proselyte entered the Jewish faith were circumcision, baptism and sacrifice. So prominent a place did baptism hold in the reception of converts to Judaism, that Rabbi Joshua argued that it alone was necessary, although he was confuted by Rabbi Eliezer.

Jewish proselyte baptism was carried out in the presence of three witnesses, if possible members of the Sanhedrin. The nails and the hair of the candidate were cut; he was stripped naked; he was completely immersed in water, so that his whole body was totally covered; the essence of the law was read to him, and he was warned of the difficulties and the dangers and the possible persecution which lay ahead; he confessed his sins to the men who were known as 'the fathers of baptism', and who correspond to godparents; then after blessings and exhortations he emerged a Jew. This process was held to effect in him the most radical change. He was said to emerge as 'a little child just born', 'a child of one day'. So completely was he a new man that it was theoretically argued that a proselyte who had been baptized might marry his own sister or his own mother, because for him the connection with the past was completely broken. Jewish proselyte baptism was no doubt founded on the many washings which the Jewish law laid down for the purposes of purification (cf. Lev. 15.5,8,13,16; 16.26,28). If washings were necessary for a Jew to cleanse the defilements he might have contracted, how much more was washing necessary for a Gentile coming from the polluted pagan world? That baptism of proselytes did exist in the time of John is proved by the record of the controversy between the famous Rabbis Hillel and Shammai. Shammai

---

[1] *The Metamorphoses* or *Golden Ass* 11.23.

held that a proselyte who was baptized on the eve of the Passover might share in the Passover Feast, while Hillel held that so quick an entry to the sacred meal was impossible. Certainly John would know of proselyte baptism, although, as we shall later see, no such baptism had ever been undergone by Jews themselves.

It is not difficult to find antecedents for John's practice of baptism. It is not suggested that John was dependent on any of them, but it is certain that John came into a situation in which baptism was known and practised. But can we go further and can we find any antecedents for John himself?

When Josephus was describing the great Jewish sects and parties, he described the Pharisees and the Sadducees, and then he described what he called the third of the Jewish sects, the Essenes. Our information regarding these Essenes comes from three sources, from Philo's *Quod omnis probus liber* 12,13, from the elder Pliny's *Natural History* 5.17, from Josephus' *Wars of the Jews* 2.8.2-13, and from his *Antiquities* 13.5.9; 15.10.4,5; 18.1.5.

It is in fact hardly right to class the Essenes as parallel with the Pharisees and the Sadducees. The Pharisees and the Sadducees were by no means withdrawn from the world, and they were, at least to some extent, political parties as well as religious sects, but, as Schürer rightly says in *The Jewish People in the Time of Christ*, the Essenes were rather a monastic order. They seem to have come into being somewhere midway through the second century BC. They could be found in small groups in the villages and in the towns, but they found their real life and their real flowering living in communities, closely disciplined and closely organized. The main site of their community life was in the Desert of Engedi near the Dead Sea. To enter an Essene community was an act of spontaneous and deliberate choice. The candidate was first on a year's probation; he was then admitted to their washings and lustrations; he had another two years' probation; he was then admitted to the common meal, which was a feature of their communal life, and he then took the terrible and awe-inspiring oath that his whole life would be open to the brethren, but absolutely secret to the outsider.

Their communities were ascetic and their discipline was very strict. They practised absolute community of goods, so that amongst them, as Josephus says, there was neither 'the humiliation of poverty or the superfluity of wealth'. Even the desire to have anything of one's own did not exist among them. Thus sickness and old age lost their terrors among the Essenes, for the ill and the aged received from the common pool all that they needed.

Their way of life was very simple. Their work lay mainly in agriculture. They knew the healing properties of plants and stones. All trading was forbidden, for trading, so they said, leads to covetousness; they were pledged to make no weapons of warfare and to make nothing which could be used to harm anyone else. They were famous for the goodness of their lives, 'abstemious, simple, unpretending', as Schürer describes them.

They possessed no slaves. They took no oaths. They used no anointing oil. They wore white garments. They were meticulously careful in what we would now call matters of hygiene. They were extraordinarily modest in regard to the display of the naked body. They were celibate. They made no animal sacrifices, although, it is said, they sent incense to the Temple. All their meals were common meals; all were prepared by a priest; and before all meals there were careful washings and purificatory rites. They had a kind of passion for cleanliness. The most characteristic thing about their practices was their numerous washings. They bathed themselves in cold water before every meal; they bathed always after the performance of their natural functions; they bathed always after any contact with anyone less meticulous than themselves.

They had a strong belief in providence, or even in fate. They read and studied the Scriptures, and used them at their worship, at which they delighted in allegorical interpretations. They had a supreme reverence for the law and for Moses. the law-giver.

They had certain practices and beliefs which were curiously un-Jewish. First thing in the morning they prayed facing the sun, as if somewhere in their history and beliefs there had been some admixture of sun worship. They believed in the immortality of the soul, but not of the body; for they believed the soul to be pre-existent, and to be imprisoned in the prison house of the body. Thus death was the liberation of the soul, and the destruction of the body, for those who had lived and worshipped aright. This dualism of body and soul is not Jewish, and may have come to them from the East.

It has been suggested that it was from these Essenes that John the Baptizer came. They had their principal community in the very wilderness in which he must have grown up. Josephus (*Wars of the Jews* 2.8.2) says of the Essenes: 'Marriage they disdain, but they adopt other men's children, while yet pliable and docile, and regard them as their kin, and mould them in accordance with their principles.' The suggestion has been made that the Essene community adopted John while he was still a child. His parents were aged when he was born (Luke 1.7), and John may well have been left an orphan very young. So it is suggested that John may have grown up amongst these simple, ascetic, disciplined, pious people, who lived in their daily ritual of cleansing washings, and that it may have been from them that he took his uncompromising ethical demand, and also the cleansing washing of his baptism.

The connection of John with the Essenes is no new idea, but recent discoveries have revived and intensified the idea of this connection. It was in 1947 that there happened the accidental discovery of the first batch of these ancient documents popularly known as the Dead Sea Scrolls. They represent the books and the libraries of a community, perhaps four thousand in number, who lived in the ravine of Qumran at the north end of the Dead Sea. This community bears the strongest possible resemblance to the Essenes; in fact they may well be identified with the Essenes. This community believed that the covenant between God and Israel had always throughout history been preserved and maintained by some faithful remnant. They had withdrawn themselves from ordinary life, for they believed themselves to be the faithful remnant, who alone understood the true meaning of the law, a meaning which had been passed down to them through a series of Right-teachers or Teachers of Righteousness, who were also priests. They were awaiting the new Prophet and Teacher who would announce the new and golden age in which there would come to men God's anointed Priest and God's anointed King.

What we are here concerned with, and what we must here

confine ourselves to, is the possible connection of John the Baptizer with this Qumran community. There are certain striking resemblances—and equally striking differences within the resemblances—between John and the Qumran community as their beliefs and practices and ideals are set out in their *Manual of Discipline*, which is one of the documents which have been discovered. We quote this in the version of Theodor H. Gaster, entitled *The Scriptures of the Dead Sea Sect*. The members of this community are to sever their connection with ordinary men 'to the end that they may indeed "go into the wilderness to prepare the way", i.e. do what Scripture enjoins when it says, "Prepare in the wilderness the way . . . make straight in the desert a highway for our God" (Isa 40.3). The reference is to the study of the Law which God commanded Moses to the end that, as occasion arises, all things may be done in accordance with what is revealed therein and with what the prophets have revealed through God's holy spirit.'[1] The extraordinary fact is that the aim of this Qumran community is expressed in the very words of Isaiah which the New Testament writers use to describe the function of John the Baptizer (Matt. 3.3; Mark 1.3; Luke 3.4).

But with the resemblance there is a difference. It was for *themselves* that the Qumran community were preparing the way; they had deliberately separated themselves from men in order to prepare the way. If John was connected with them, he must have grown discontented with this narrow, confined, and even selfish preparation, and must have left them to strike out on the preparation, not of a sect or a community, but of a nation.

Further, in the *Manual of Discipline* there is the closest possible connection between the idea of cleansing ritually by water and the amendment of life. It is more than once insisted that the ritual cleansing is useless unless moral cleansing accompanies it. So it is said of the man who insists on walking 'in the stubbornness of his heart':

> He cannot be cleared by mere ceremonies of atonement, nor cleansed by any waters of ablution, nor sanctified by immersion in lakes or rivers, nor purified by any bath. Unclean, unclean

---

[1] *Manual of Discipline* 8.13ff.

he remains so long as he rejects the government of God, and refuses the discipline of communion with him. For it is only through the spiritual apprehension of God's truth that man's ways can be properly directed. Only thus can all his iniquities be shriven so that he can gaze on the true light of life. Only through the holy spirit can he achieve union with God's truth and be purged of all his iniquities. Only by a spirit of uprightness and humility can his sin be atoned. Only by the submission of his soul to all the ordinances of God can his flesh be made clean. Only thus can it be sprinkled with waters of ablution.[1]

It is said of God in the recreated age: 'Like waters of purification God will sprinkle upon him (the good man) the spirit of truth.'[2] It is laid down: 'No one is to go into water in order to attain the purity of holy men. For men cannot be purified except they repent their evil.'[3] There is the closest connection between the demand of the Qumran community for holiness and the ethical demand of John.

It may well be that John had some connection with the Essenes, and that he even had some connection with the Qumran community. If he had, like so many great men he surpassed the origins from which he came. If he had not, it at least remains true that John delivered his message to men who had been at least to some extent prepared to understand it by the teaching of the Essenes and of men who lived in the life and held the belief of such communities as the community of Qumran.

However these things may be, the day came when John emerged from the desert with a message which was a shock to Jewish ears. He came with a *summons to repentance* (Mark. 1.4; Matt. 3.2; Luke 3.3). The reign of God was about to invade the earth, and men must repent and be cleansed before the irruption of eternity into time. He came to summon sinners to repentance. He came with a *summons to preparation*. As the prophet Isaiah had done long ago (Isa. 40.3), he came with a summons to men to prepare the way of the Lord (Matt. 3.3; Mark 1.3; Luke 3.4-6). In the ancient days all roads were 'the king's highway'. When

[1]   *Manual* 3.4ff.
[2]   *Manual* 4.21.
[3]   *Manual* 5.13.

a ruler intended to go upon a journey or to visit a district, he sent ahead messengers with orders that the roads by which he intended to travel should be smoothed and repaired, for unsurfaced roads soon degenerated into rutted tracks, and would be allowed to remain so unless the king was to come. It was John's message that the King was on the way, and the road must be prepared for him. John's message was a message which pointed beyond himself to the one whose herald he was.

He came with an *uncompromising ethical demand*. His message struck at the very roots of comfortable Jewish orthodoxy. The Jews never lost the conviction that they were the chosen people, but they interpreted their chosenness in terms of privilege rather than in terms of responsibility. There were many who held that physical descent from Abraham was enough to ensure for a man the favour of God and salvation and the right of entry into heaven, no matter what kind of life he had lived. They could actually say that at the gate of hell there was stationed a kind of guardian angel to turn back any Jew who had the mark of circumcision in his flesh, and who had in error strayed there. Descent from Abraham was the passport to the favour of God. That was a belief on which John poured a withering scorn (Matt. 3.7-9; Luke 3.7f.). He insisted that what mattered was a man's character, and therefore he came with his absolute ethical demand. The rich must share with the poor; the tax-collector must be an honest man; the soldier must be a man under honourable discipline; a man must live the good life wherever God had set him (Luke 3.10-14). And so in the end John came with a *threat*. The Greater One was coming; the axe was poised to smite the fruitless tree; the chaff was to be winnowed from the grain; the time of judgment was on the way (Matt. 3.11f.; Luke 3.9,16f.).

The message of John swept across the minds of the people like a blast of wind from heaven, because there were certain unique characteristics in it. Four things stood out in the message and the personality of John.

(i) In him the prophetic voice spoke again. The Jews wistfully and regretfully acknowledged that for three hundred years the voice of prophecy had been silent. The priest might sacrifice; the rabbi might teach and expound the law; but the authentic voice of prophecy spoke no more. But in John men recognized once again that accent and that authority with which the prophets had spoken.

(ii)　John's summons was a summons to repentance. The Jews themselves had a saying: 'If Israel repent but for a single day, forthwith the Redeemer will come.' Here was the summons to that godly sorrow and that cleansing of life which were the essential prelude to the coming of the King.

(iii)　It was a fixed part of Jewish belief—and still is—that Elijah would return to be the herald of the coming of the Messiah and of the last times. Malachi heard the voice of God saying: 'Behold, I will send you Elijah the prophet, before the great and terrible day of the Lord comes' (Mal. 4.5). John's very clothes were the clothes which Elijah had worn (Mark 1.6; Matt. 3.4; II Kings 1.8). The accent of his voice was the accent of Elijah. Men could not but see in John the coming again of Elijah as the herald of the end.

(iv)　But there was one completely unique feature of the ministry of John. John summoned the people to repent and to be baptized in order to receive forgiveness for their sins. *Never in history had a Jew been baptized*. Baptism was something not for Jew but for a Gentile. It was true that, when a Gentile came into Judaism as a proselyte, then he was baptized, for he needed to be washed and cleansed from the evil of his Gentile ways. That was natural and necessary for a Gentile, but no one had ever conceived that a Jew should need baptism, and that a member of the chosen people should need to submit to a cleansing process such as that. As Plummer puts it: 'John had excommunicated the whole nation.' John's summons was to men as sinners, who, even if they were Jews, desperately needed and passionately desired the cleansing which God alone could give. The unique fact about John was that John summoned the Jews to undergo baptism for their cleansing from sin, an unheard of thing for a Jew to do—and the Jews came in their hundreds to accept John's demand.

So when John emerged from the desert with his summons to repentance and to baptism, and when the people flocked out to the Jordan to be baptized, Jesus came too, because Jesus knew that for him the hour had struck. Here there is a problem which has exercised the minds of men ever since they began to study the New Testament. Why should Jesus be baptized? John's baptism was very definitely and very directly a mark of repentance, and it was designed for the cleansing of men so that their sins might be forgiven. What need of repentance had Jesus, the sinless one? What need had he of a baptism which was the mark of repentance, and the symbol of cleansing from sin, in order that men might be forgiven?

Even in the narratives of the four Gospels this difficulty and this problem lurk beneath the surface. John omits the story of the baptism altogether. For Mark the problem has not yet arisen. Mark describes John's baptism as 'a baptism of repentance for the forgiveness of sins' (1.4), and goes on simply to say that Jesus came from Nazareth of Galilee and was baptized by John in the Jordan (1.9). Luke also describes John's baptism as 'a baptism of repentance for the forgiveness of sins' (3.3); he tells how Jesus came to be baptized and was baptized (3.21), but he takes care to make John bear witness to the absolute supremacy of Jesus (3.15f.). But it is Matthew who feels the problem most acutely. He tells us that John came with the summons to repent for the Kingdom of God is at hand, but he does not mention that the baptism was for the remission of sins (3.1). He cannot bring himself to connect such a baptism with Jesus. He goes on to tell how Jesus came and how John at first refused to baptize him, and how Jesus said that all righteousness must be fulfilled (3.13-15). The very way in which the Gospel writers tell the story show how difficult Matthew especially found the baptism of Jesus by John to be. Let us then look at some of the explanations which have been suggested.

The oldest explanation is found in two writings of the early Church. It is that Jesus was baptized, almost against his will, and to please his mother and his family. Jerome[1] preserves a brief fragment of the lost *Gospel according to the Hebrews:* 'Behold, the mother of the Lord and his brothers said to him: John the Baptizer baptizes unto the remission of sins; let us go and be baptized by him. But he said to them: Wherein have I sinned, that I should go and be baptized by him? unless perhaps this very

[1] *Dialogue against Pelagius* 3.2.

thing that I have said is a sin of ignorance.' An anonymous writer tells us that the lost *Preaching of Paul* speaks of 'Christ, the only man who was altogether without fault, both making confession respecting his own sin, and driven almost against his will by his mother Mary to accept the baptism of John'.[1] There may possibly be something in this, to which we shall return, but these two ancient accounts show us Jesus accepting baptism to please his family, and almost against his will.

It has been suggested that Jesus was baptized by John as the representative of mankind. This is how Justin Martyr saw the baptism: 'We know that he did not go to the river because he stood in need of baptism, or of the descent of the Spirit like a dove; even as he submitted to be born and to be crucified, not because he needed such things, but because of the human race, which from Adam had fallen under the power of death and the guile of the serpent, and each one of which had committed personal transgression.'[2] This view sees Jesus as making an act of repentance and of submission to God as the representative of all mankind. It is as if he brought to God for all men a perfect penitence and a perfect obedience.

It has been suggested that the baptism of Jesus was a fulfilment of prophecy. In Isaiah (11.2) we read of the promised King, 'The Spirit of the Lord shall rest upon him,' and the events of the baptism may be taken as a fulfilment of that prophecy. There was a Jewish tradition that the Messiah would not know himself and would not have any power until Elijah came to anoint him. It is possible to see in the baptism the fulfilment of the events which the prophets had foretold about the chosen one of God.

There may be truth in all these views, but we believe that the real meaning of the baptism is that for Jesus it was a deliberate act of self-identification with men. In the baptism Jesus identified himself with men in four different ways.

(i) He identified himself with men in their search for righteousness. When John refused at first to baptize him, Jesus told him to do so in order to fulfil all righteousness (Matt. 3.15).

---

[1] *Tractate on Rebaptism* 17.
[2] *Dialogue with Trypho* 88.

Those who came to be baptized were earnestly seeking to do God's will, and with that seeking Jesus identified himself.

(ii)   He identified himself with men in their preparation for the breaking-in of God. For the Jews baptism by John was an act of preparation for the coming of the Kingdom, and Jesus joined in that preparation, for he was to bring the Kingdom.

(iii)   He identified himself with men in their search for God. It was because men heard in John the voice of God that they flocked out to the Jordan to him. This crowd of people were searchers after God, and Jesus identified himself with them.

(iv)   But we have not yet come to the deepest level of the meaning of the baptism. In the baptism Jesus identified himself with the sin and the sorrow of mankind. These Jews came to John as sinners; they came because a sense of sin drove them, and because they were made to feel as never before their need of God and their need of the forgiveness of God, and it was precisely with sinful men that Jesus identified himself. He made, as it has been put, 'common cause with all men in life in the mortal dilemma'. George A. Buttrick quotes the story of a man who in the time of his wife's infidelity, when he was in no way to blame, came to her and said: 'Since you and I have done this . . .' Such was his love that, even when the sin was not his own, he identified himself with the sinner, with the penitence and with the sorrow. In the baptism Jesus the sinless identified himself with sinful men. He took upon himself their sorrow, their contrition, their search for God; he became one in heart with the men whom he had come to save; he became, as Irenaeus put it, what we are to make us what he is.[1]

For Jesus himself the event of the baptism was a great occasion. There is little doubt that for Jesus the baptism was far more a private and personal experience than it was a public demonstration. The words of the voice at the baptism are given in two forms. Matthew has: '*This* is my beloved Son' (Matt. 3.17), as if Jesus was being pointed out by the divine voice to all who were there to see. But both Mark and Luke have: '*Thou* art my beloved Son' (Mark 1.11; Luke 3.22), as if to say that the words came to Jesus and to Jesus alone. The events of the baptism did not happen for the sake of the crowd; they happened for the

[1]   *Against Heresies*, Prologue to Book 5.

sake of Jesus himself. So, then, for Jesus the baptism was certain quite definite things.

It was for him *the moment of decision*. As Rawlinson puts it: 'Jesus recognized his appointed hour.' It was the moment when he decided once and for all to cut the cables and to launch out into the deep. The prologue gave place to the main act of the drama; the preparation was ended and the task had begun.

It was for Jesus *the moment of assurance*. Deep within his inmost being he received the ultimate and unshakable certainty that he was, as no man had ever been or could ever be, the Son of God. Now here is where there may well be some kind of hint of truth behind the very early stories which tell of Jesus as being unwilling to go to John, and as going under pressure from his family. We have already seen the account of what happened which is in the *Gospel according to the Hebrews*. In that Gospel Jesus' words are: 'Wherein have I sinned, that I should go and be baptized by John? unless peradventure this very thing that I have said is a sin of ignorance.' The strange thing is that in that saying of Jesus there is a lurking doubt and uncertainty; Jesus in it recognizes the possibility that he may be mistaken. Two things are clear, and these two things must be set side by side. First, Jesus so identified himself with men that he entered absolutely and completely into the human situation. Second, a part of the human situation, which no one who has set his hand to some great task fully escapes, is self-doubt. To every man there comes the moment or moments when in his heart and soul there is a little shiver of doubt, a faint question mark, the terrible feeling that maybe he may be mistaken, the grim realization of the possibility that he may be on the wrong road. If these two facts are so, then Jesus did not fully enter into the human situation, unless at some time there were deep in his heart the self-doubtings and the self-questionings which are part of the heritage of the human spirit. The baptism was the moment when the last of these doubts perished for ever. In that moment there came to him such an experience of the fatherhood of God and of his own sonship, such an utter conviction of the approval of God, such a certainty of God's will for him, that he never doubted himself or his task again.

It so happens that certain of the Greek manuscripts have in

Luke a variant reading in the sentence which contains the words of God. The best manuscripts all read: 'Thou art my beloved Son; with thee I am well pleased.' But the so-called Western Text reads: 'Thou art my beloved Son; *today I have begotten thee,*' which is indeed the full text of Ps. 2.7. If that were the true reading, it would mean that in that moment the man Jesus was fully and finally chosen for the work which God brought him into the world to do; it would mean that all through the long thirty years of preparation Jesus had so proved and prepared himself that now in this tremendous moment God was adopting him into unique sonship for a unique task; it would mean that in that moment God offered and Jesus accepted the supreme task of being the Saviour of the world.

In any event, the one thing that is certain is that for Jesus the baptism was the moment of assurance, when there came to him the utter certainty that the way ahead was clear.

It was for him *the moment of equipment.* In the most unique way the Holy Spirit of God came upon him (Mark 1.10; Matt. 3.16; Luke 3.22). Once again the implication of the narrative is that this was an experience which was personal and private to Jesus. Here is something that a Jew could understand. Again and again the coming of the Spirit of God was the preparation and the equipment of a man for some great task. It was so with Othniel (Judg. 3.10); with Gideon (Judg. 6.34); with Jephthah (Judg. 11.29); with Samson (Judg. 13.25); with Saul (I Sam. 10.10); with the king anointed by God (Isa. 11.2); with the Servant of God (Isa. 42.1). But in the case of Jesus there was a difference. In the case of the others the coming of the Spirit was the preparation for *a special task*; it was, so to speak, a temporary equipment; the tide of the Spirit flowed but the tide of the Spirit also ebbed; the flame blazed and the flame flickered. But in the case of Jesus the coming of the Spirit was an equipment *for life*; it was the permanent indwelling of the Spirit in him. A surviving fragment of the *Gospel according to the Hebrews,* preserved by Jerome in his commentary on Isa. 11.2, seems to seize upon this very point: 'And it came to pass, when the Lord was come up out of the water, *the whole fount of the Holy Spirit descended and rested upon him,* and said unto him: My Son, in all the prophets was I waiting for thee that thou shouldst come, and *I might rest in thee*. For thou art my rest, thou art my first-begotten Son, that reignest for ever.' It was no portion of the Spirit which came upon Jesus; it was the very fountain of the Spirit. It was no temporary gift of the Spirit; it was the permanent abiding of the Spirit in him. In the moment of the baptism Jesus was divinely equipped for his task.

Great as these things are, the baptism had a significance for Jesus which was still greater and still deeper. For him it was at one and the same time *the moment of enlightenment* and *the moment of self-dedication*. The voice which came to Jesus said: 'Thou art my beloved Son; with thee I am well pleased' (Mark 1.11; Matt. 3.17; Luke 3.22). That saying is composed of two sayings from the Old Testament. 'Thou art my beloved Son' is a quotation from Ps. 2.7. Ps. 2 is a description of a testing time in the life of the king of the holy nation. The heathen rage and rebel; but the king can have perfect confidence, because God has taken him as his son, and his cause is safe in the hands and in the power and in the promise of God. Not only will his own realm be safe and his own throne secure and his immediate enemies conquered and subdued; the day will come when God will extend his kingdom to the ends of the earth. No doubt when that psalm was first composed and sung it was meant for a definite situation in history when the throne of Israel was in peril; but, as the days went on, that psalm came to be regarded as a messianic psalm and as a prophecy and foretelling of the triumph of the Messiah, the anointed King of God. So, then, when Jesus heard this voice, he knew himself to be the Messiah, the King sent by God to be the Lord of men and the ruler of the earth. Here is the forecast of ultimate victory and of universal triumph.

But there was a second clause in the words which came to Jesus in the divine voice—'with thee I am well pleased.' That is a quotation from Isa. 42.1: 'Behold my servant, whom I uphold, my chosen, *in whom my soul delights.*' That is part of the picture of the Servant of the Lord, of the great and mysterious figure whose portrait culminates in Isa. 53, of the one who was wounded for our transgressions and bruised for our iniquities, the one on whom the chastisement of our peace fell, the one who was to be like a sheep dumb before its shearers. When Jesus heard these words, he must have realized with blinding certainty that his ultimate victory was certain, but that the way to it was the way of sorrow, of suffering, of sacrificial service, of self-dedication as an offering for the sins of men.

So when Jesus heard the voice, he knew that he was God's chosen Messiah, but he also knew that the way for him was the way of the Cross.

In the baptism we see the self-identification of Jesus with men and the self-dedication of Jesus to the purposes of God.

In Justin Martyr's account of the baptism there is one strange addition to the story. Justin says: 'And then, when Jesus had gone to the river Jordan, where John was baptizing, and when he had stepped into the water, a fire was kindled in Jordan.'[1] This fire is also mentioned in the *Gospel according to the Hebrews*. Where Justin and that Gospel got the story we do not know and we cannot tell. But the story is symbolically true, for in that moment of the baptism there was kindled in the heart of Jesus a flame of sacrificial love which nothing in time or in eternity could ever extinguish.

[1] *Dialogue with Trypho* 88.

4

CHOOSING HIS WAY

THERE have been those who have dismissed the story of the temptations of Jesus as completely unhistorical. Guignebert, for instance, describes it as 'completely legendary', 'sheer hagiographical imagination', 'all too obvious fiction'. But the plain fact is that, whatever may be said about the form of the temptation story, its events are absolutely necessary, if we are to make sense of the life of Jesus. It represents an essential step in the line of his life.

For years Jesus had waited in Nazareth, undergoing the long preparation for his task. With the emergence of John the Baptizer he knew that for him the hour had struck, and the time to begin had come. In the moment of the baptism Jesus received assurance, equipment, enlightenment to go on. And thereupon one decision was necessarily forced upon Jesus. He knew now what his task was; he knew what he had come into the world to do. He was the Messiah, the Chosen One of God; he must bring to men the Kingdom of God. And the immediate question was— *How?* How was he to set about this task? What methods was he to use? What way was he to pursue? It is to these questions that Jesus found his answer in the events of the temptation story. To be given a task is to be obliged to find a method to carry it out. Jesus had been given his task; and now in the events of his temptation he decided on the method which he must follow. For Jesus this decision was all the more necessary and all the more difficult in that there already existed a popular picture of the Messiah as the triumphant liberator of the Jewish people, the conqueror of Rome, and victorious overlord of all the earth. The choice before Jesus was whether he was to fit himself into the popular messianic pattern or strike out upon a way that was his own. It was to make that choice that Jesus went into the lonely places to fight his personal battle with the voices which called him to the wrong way. Before we begin to study the meaning for Jesus of the events of the temptation story, there are certain general facts which we must note.

We must be clear as to the meaning of the word *temptation* as it is used in this story and in the Bible generally. For the most part we regard temptation as a deliberate and malevolent attempt to seduce a man into sin. But in the New Testament the word *(peirazein)* means much more 'to test' than 'to tempt'. In this story of the temptations of Jesus the Gospel writers are unanimous that it was the Holy Spirit who led Jesus into the desert places (Mark 1.12; Matt. 4.1; Luke 4.1). If we regard temptation simply as an attempt to seduce a man into sin, that would mean that the Holy Spirit was actually a partner in an assault on the purity and the goodness of Jesus. In the Old Testament story which tells of Abraham and Isaac we read: 'And it came to pass after these things that God did *tempt* Abraham' (Gen. 22.1, AV). If we take the word 'tempt' in nothing more than the sense of seduction into sin, we are left with an incredible situation in which God sought to persuade Abraham to sin. The difficulty vanishes immediately when we substitute the word 'test' for the word 'tempt'. God was *testing* Abraham. The *temptation* of Jesus was the *testing* of Jesus. Temptation is always a testing; it is not meant to make a man fall; it is meant to test him and to try him, so that out of the testing situation he will emerge stronger and finer and purer, like a metal that is tested and tried in the fire.

The temptation story is the strongest proof that Jesus was conscious of possessing special and wonderful powers. It would be no temptation to an ordinary person to change stones into bread or to leap down unharmed from the Temple pinnacle. Unless his mind was unhinged with the delusion of grandeur, he would know that he could not do these things. The temptation story is the story of a person who was aware that he possessed special powers, and who was faced with the suggestion that he should use these powers in the wrong way.

The method of the tempter is very revealing. None of the courses which he suggested was obviously evil. There is surely nothing obviously wrong in turning stones into bread; there is surely nothing wrong in demonstrating the care of God for his own by taking some adventurous and dangerous course of action; there is surely nothing wrong in an action which will win over the whole world. If temptation was obviously evil, if the result of falling to temptation was obviously disastrous, no one would ever fall. In the old story of the temptation in the Garden of Eden the forbidden fruit which the tempter urged Eve to eat was good for food, pleasant to the eyes, and to be desired to make one wise (Gen. 3.6). The subtlety of temptation is that it suggests a course of action which is on the face of it attractive and advantageous. The power of temptation lies in the fact that so often evil can look like good—to him who takes only the short-term view of life.

When we think of the temptation story, and when we think of what was happening to Jesus, we must not think in terms of a series of external scenes. We must think of a struggle that was going on in the inmost heart and being and soul of Jesus, an inner agony of choice and decision. It is true that there are some—Bengel was one—who thought that Satan always works through human agencies, and who imagined that what happened was that some emissary or some deputation of the Sanhedrin followed Jesus out into the desert, and attempted to persuaded him to embark upon the role of the conquering Messiah, and so to fulfil popular expectation and gain popular support. That is not what we are to think of. We are to think of a long struggle in the deeps of the being of Jesus, going on continuously until for the time being he gained the victory. Nor are we to think of this as a final victory. Luke tells us at the end of the story that the devil departed for a season (4.13,AV), until an opportune time (RSV). The whole story is a vivid way of describing the inner battle in the heart and mind and soul of Jesus, a battle which lasted until the end of the day.

There is one fact which sets this story in a class by itself among Gospel stories. The story can have had only one source; it can have come from none other than Jesus himself. He was alone in the desert; it was his own private and personal and inmost struggle; and the story of it can have come from nowhere else than from his own lips. The day must have come when he told it to his disciples for their warning, their comfort and their strengthening. This story is, therefore, one of the most sacred in the whole Gospel narrative.

There remains one other thing which it is essential to say. The tempting of Jesus was a real tempting. To put it in technical terms, there is an old argument as to whether we are to think of Jesus in terms of *non posse peccare* or *posse non peccare*; that is to say, whether we are to say that it was *not possible for him to sin,* or that it was *possible for him not to sin.* There have always been some who in a mistaken reverence have held that there was no possibility of Jesus falling to temptation, that he was of such complete goodness and purity, that he was, so to speak, so much God that he could not possibly have fallen to temptation. To believe that is to make the temptation story quite unreal, and to reduce it to a kind of play-acting. We must have no 'doubt of the utter reality of the temptation of Jesus; and, when we realize this, the temptation story becomes one of the most dramatic stories in history, for in those days when Jesus was tempted and tested, the fate of God's plan of salvation was literally swinging in the balance. It is further true that Jesus was not tempted less but more than any other person. In the case of ordinary men like ourselves, the tempter never has to put out his full power; we fall long before that; but in the case of Jesus the tempter put forth every effort he could, and Jesus overcame them all. To Jesus there came a strength and violence of temptation which no one else has ever known—and he overcame.

So, then, Jesus had come to the all-important moment when he had to choose how he would approach the work which God had given him to do. Jesus sought no human advice; he went away to be alone to settle the problem and to think the matter out. It was into 'the wilderness' that he went.

The wilderness was the Wilderness of Judaea, which stretches from the hill country south of Jerusalem down to the Dead Sea. It covers an area of thirty-five by fifteen miles, and in the Old Testament its name is Jeshimmon, which means 'The Devastation'. Sir George Adam Smith describes it in *The Historical Geography of the Holy Land:* 'The strata were contorted; ridges ran in all directions; distant hills to north and south looked like gigantic dust-heaps; those near we could see to be torn as if by waterspouts. When we were not stepping on detritus, the limestone was blistered and peeling. Often the ground sounded hollow; sometimes rock and sand slipped in large quantities from the tread of the horses; sometimes the living rock was bare and jagged, especially in the frequent gullies, that therefore glowed and beat with heat like furnaces.' It was into that grim and bleak loneliness that Jesus went to make his great decision.

For forty days Jesus was alone (Mark 1.13; Matt. 4.2; Luke 4.2). The forty days is not to be taken with time-table-like literalness. It was for forty days that the rains preceded the Flood (Gen. 7.12); it was for forty days that Moses was on Mount Sinai (Ex. 24.18), and that Elijah was in the wilderness (I Kings 19.8). It is to be taken simply as expressing a long period of time.

Mark (1.13) tells us that Jesus was with the wild beasts. It may be that Mark adds this detail to add further grim loneliness to the scene, as if painting a picture of a wilderness in which no human foot trod and there were only the beasts. But it also may be that Mark is thinking of the new covenant in which man and the beasts will be fearless friends together (Hos. 2.18), and that he is thinking of the beasts, not as threatening Jesus, but as being his companions in the wilderness loneliness, in which case the picture would be a picture of loveliness and not of terror.

During this time Jesus was fasting (Matt. 4.2; Luke 4.2), and a time of fasting like that necessarily heightens a man's mental and spiritual perceptiveness and awareness.

The story of the temptations is told in Mark 1.12f., Matt. 4.1-11 and Luke 4.1-13. Mark gives us no detail at all. In Matthew and Luke the order of the temptations is different. In Matthew the order is, first, to turn the stones into bread; second, to leap down unharmed from the pinnacle of the Temple; third, to worship Satan and so to gain the lordship of the kingdoms of the world. In Luke the order of the second and third temptations is reversed. It does not make any real difference, and we shall use Matthew's order as the basis of our study. Let us first look at the actual temptations themselves before we seek to study their meaning and their significance for Jesus.

The first temptation was the temptation to turn the stones into bread (Matt. 4.3f.; Luke 4.3f.). What temptation could be more natural to a man who had fasted for forty days, especially when the little pieces of limestone rock with which the desert was covered were exactly like little round loaves of bread? Had not God said: 'I will rain bread from heaven for you' (Ex. 16.4)? Was not the promise: 'They shall not hunger or thirst'

(Isa. 49.10)? But Jesus countered this temptation with the words of the law: 'Man shall not live by bread alone, but by every word that proceeds from the mouth of God' (Deut. 8.3).

In the second temptation Jesus in imagination saw himself on 'the pinnacle of the Temple', and the temptation was to leap down, and to land and at the foot of it unharmed (Luke 4.9-12; Matt. 4.5-7). 'The pinnacle of the Temple' may be either of two places. On the south side of the Temple rose the Royal Porch. The outer wall of the Royal Porch rose straight up from the side of the hill on which Jerusalem and the Temple were built. There was a sheer drop of four hundred and fifty feet to the Kedron valley below, a drop so famous and notorious that Josephus tells us that no one could look down it without being overcome with dizziness.[1] Edersheim has another suggestion to make. The first great event of the Temple day was the morning sacrifice which had to be made as soon as dawn came. There was a tall tower in the Temple, on the top of which a priest was stationed with a silver trumpet to sound the blast upon it when the first streaks of dawn came across the hills, and so to tell all men that the time of sacrifice had come. At such a time the Temple court would be thronged with expectant worshippers, with their eyes fixed on the priest who waited to give the signal that the dawn had come. If Jesus chose to leap down from the top of that tower at that moment he would indeed have an audience for his miracle of sensation.

This, then, was the second temptation which came to Jesus. Had not God promised: 'He will give his angels charge of you,' and, 'On their hands they will bear you up, lest you strike your foot against a stone' (Ps. 91.11f.)? But once again Jesus countered temptation with a word from the law: 'You shall not tempt the Lord your God' (Deut. 6.16).

In the third temptation Jesus saw himself on a high mountain from which all the kingdoms of the earth could be seen. Of course there is no mountain from which the whole world may be seen; but here the *Gospel according to the Hebrews* has an interesting addition. It identifies the mountain as Mount Tabor, the very mountain from whose summit Jesus may well

[1]   *Antiquities* 15.11.5.

have looked on the world and its roads, when he was a boy.

Was not the promise of God: 'Ask of me, and I will make the nations your heritage, and the ends of the earth your possession' (Ps. 2.8)? So the tempter tempted Jesus to strike a bargain with him, and all these nations would be his. But again Jesus countered temptation with a word from the law: 'You shall worship the Lord your God and him only shall you serve' (Deut. 6.13).

So Jesus vanquished temptation; but the battle was not over. As Luke has it, the tempter, though defeated on this occasion, departed from him until an opportune time (Luke 4.13). For Jesus, as for all men, the battle with the tempter is never wholly won until the very end of the day.

Before we examine the three temptations in detail, we must note that in them the tempter made one basic attack on Jesus. He attacked Jesus' consciousness of himself and of his task. 'If you are the Son of God,' he began (Matt. 4.3,5; Luke 4.3,9). This was an attack which was to return even when Jesus was on the cross. 'If you are the Son of God,' said his enemies, 'come down from the cross' (Matt. 27.40; Luke 23.35-37). Here is the temptation to Jesus to distrust himself, to doubt his call, to question his task and his ability and equipment for it. It is as if the tempter said: 'How can you, a penniless, uneducated, Galilaean carpenter, possibly be the Messiah of God? Who ever conceived of a Messiah starving in a wilderness? Who ever thought of a Messiah on the way to a cross?' There is nothing so paralysing as doubt; there can be no decisive and effective action without certainty. Jesus well knew the traditional and conventional ideas of what the Messiah ought to be; and he well knew that the way he was called upon to choose was a complete and revolutionary contradiction of them. The tempter began by seeking to make Jesus doubt his own call from God, but Jesus was so sure of God, and of his own relationship to God, that the attack failed.

Let us now take each temptation by itself and study its meaning.

(i) There was the temptation to turn the stones into bread. There were two temptations there.

(a) It was the temptation to use his power selfishly. After all, Jesus might well say: 'My response to the summons of God has lost me my job and my living. I was once a reasonably well-to-do carpenter, and now I am a homeless wanderer. Why should I not use my powers to satisfy my own needs?' Here was the temptation to use power for himself and not for others.

(b) It was the temptation to attempt to win men by material gifts, and so to bribe them into becoming his followers, a temptation which was all the more acute because of the dreams of prosperity and plenty which did attach themselves to the messianic age. But Jesus well knew that men whose loyalty can be bought by the bribe of material gifts can just as easily be lured from their loyalty by some one who bids for their support with the offer of still more munificent gifts.

(ii) There was the temptation to leap down from the Temple pinnacle. Again there were two temptations there.

(a) There was the temptation to dazzle men with sensations. Men can always be temporarily dazzled into following a leader; but Jesus well knew that today's wonder can very easily become tomorrow's commonplace; and he who proposes to win men by sensations is committed to a course in which he must find ever more and more marvels to offer, or his followers will drift and dwindle away.

(b) But this in point of fact was a temptation which was typical of a whole attitude of mind. It was the temptation to become the kind of messianic leader who rose in Palestine again and again, the kind of leader whose one aim was to lead a sensational and successful rebellion against Rome. It is the grim fact that in Palestine between the years 67 and 37 BC no fewer than 100,000 men perished in abortive rebellions. The day was to come when Theudas was to persuade a great mass of the people to follow him out to the Jordan, with the claim that with a word he would cleave the waters in two and they would pass over dryshod,[1] only to have his followers annihilated by Cuspius Fadus, the Roman governor. The day was to come when an Egyptian impostor (Acts 21.38) was to lead hordes of the Jews out to the Mount of Olives with the promise that with a word

[1] Josephus, *Antiquities* 20.5.1.

he could cause the walls of Jerusalem to collapse, only to have his revolt crushed by Antonius Felix.[2] There had been, and were to come, any number of sensation-promising revolutionaries. They had never lacked a following and they never would lack one. Jesus was confronted with the temptation to take the way which so many would-be, self-styled saviours of their country had taken.

(iii)   There was the temptation to worship Satan, and so to enter into possession of the kingdoms of the world. That is the temptation to compromise. It is as if Satan said: 'Do not be so uncompromising; do not pitch your demands quite so high; allow men just a little more latitude; strike a bargain with me; and then they will follow you to the end.' But for Jesus there could be no compromise with anything that was less than the best, and with anything which was not completely subject to God.

The temptations which came to Jesus were the temptation to the selfish use of power, the temptation to set material benefits in the forefront of his programme, the temptation to seek for quick results by sensational means, the temptation to win popularity by compromise, and, perhaps more than anything else, the temptation to distrust himself and to doubt his call, and to accept traditional expectations rather than to listen to the voice of God. And his method of dealing with temptation was to submit every desire and every inclination to the word and the will of God, and to obey the verdict that he found there.

[2]   Josephus, *Antiquities* 20.8.6; *Wars of the Jews* 2.3.5.

5

THE BEGINNING OF THE CAMPAIGN

'J E S U S came into Galilee preaching the gospel of God' (Mark 1.14). In that one sentence Mark sets down the beginning of the campaign of Jesus.

A wise commander has to decide not only *when* to begin but also *where* to begin. The *point* of attack is at least as important as the *time* of attack. It was in Galilee that Jesus began, and there are three reasons why Galilee was a wise choice.

Galilee was the territory which Jesus knew best. It was in Galilee that he had grown to manhood; it was in Galilee that he had learned as a schoolboy and worked as a man; it was in Galilee that he had worshipped in the synagogue and worked in the carpenter's shop. He could speak to the people of Galilee because he had lived their life and understood their thoughts and spoke their speech.

Galilee was easily the most populous part of Palestine. If Jesus wished to reach the greatest number of people within the most limited area and in the shortest time, then Galilee was the place to begin. Josephus was once military governor of Palestine, and, therefore, he speaks out of intimate and personal knowledge of the country. He tells us in his autobiography that in Galilee there were 204 towns and villages,[1] none with a population of fewer than 15,000 persons.[2] That is to say, there were at least 3,000,000 people in Galilee. He tells us that, in addition to putting garrisons in nineteen fortified towns, he was able to raise an army of more than 100,000 young men.[3] These statements may sound like exaggerations, but they are made by the man who was once governor of the country, and the first is made in a letter to those who are actually to supersede him in the command in Galilee, and it is scarcely likely that in such circumstances, when his words could be so easily disproved, Jose-

[1] *Life* 45.
[2] *Wars of the Jews* 3.3.2.
[3] *Wars of the Jews* 2.20.6.

phus would be deliberately inaccurate. Burton, in his book *Un-explored Syria,* tells of standing on a spur of Lebanon, and of looking at the country just north of Galilee, and he says that in ancient times 'the land in many places must have appeared to be one continuous town'. There was no part of Palestine which could have provided Jesus with so great an audience for the message which he had come to bring.

The character and temperament of the people of Galilee were such that they were of all the inhabitants of Palestine most likely to be receptive to a new teacher and a new teaching. Judaea is tucked away in inaccessibility; Galilee was traversed by the greatest roads in the ancient world; and therefore Galilee was far more open to new ways and to new ideas than Judaea could ever be. The Galilaeans were eager, forward-looking people. 'They were ever fond of innovations,' said Josephus, 'and by nature disposed to changes, and delighted in seditions.'[1] They were ever ready to follow a leader who would begin an insurrection. They were quick in temper and given to quarrelling. 'The Galilaeans,' he said again, 'have never been destitute of courage.'[2] The Talmud says of them, 'They were ever more anxious for honour than for gain.'[3] There was a certain impulsive chivalry about the Galilaeans. Peter with all his shining virtues and with all his impulsive faults could well have sat for the portrait of a typical Galilaean. Amongst such a people Jesus would find men ready to listen and ready to thrill to a new message and a new call from God.

His own background, the number of the people, their character and their temperament and their history, made Galilee for Jesus the best of all places to open his campaign and to launch his mission among men.

The leader who will change the minds of men and who will change the world in which he lives must wisely choose his time of attack and his place of attack, but he must also have something more. He must be able to put his message into one flashing sentence, which men will immediately and unmistakably under-

[1] *Life* 17.
[2] *Wars of the Jews* 3.3.2.
[3] *Jerusalem Talmud,* Kethuboth 4.12.

stand, and which will at once penetrate into their minds and
lodge in their hearts. That is what Jesus did. He came to men
with a command and a statement, with an imperative and an
indicative. 'Repent,' he said, 'for the kingdom of heaven is at
hand' (Matt. 4.17; Mark 1.14f.). Let us look, then, first at the
imperative and then at the indicative of Jesus.

The imperative of Jesus is *Repent!* The terrible sin of Bethsaida and Chorazin and Capernaum was that they had seen his
mighty works and yet had not repented (Matt. 11.20f.; Luke
10.13-15). Men are confronted with the alternative, 'Repent or
perish' (Luke 13.3,5). The disciples are sent out to bring to men
the summons to repent (Mark 6.12). It is the repentance of the
sinner which wakens the greatest joy in heaven (Luke 15.7,10).
Clearly, if we are to understand the mind of Jesus, the meaning
of this word *repent* must be fixed and defined.

In the New Testament the word for 'repentance' is *metanoia,*
and the word for 'to repent' is *metanoein*. Both words are connected with *nous* which means 'the mind'. In this case the prefix
meta means 'after', and *noia* means 'a thought'. Therefore, the
basic meaning of *metanoia* is 'an afterthought'. The classical
writers sometimes contrast *metanoia*, 'afterthought', with *pronoia*, 'forethought', saying that the wise man exercises forethought, *pronoia*, and has not to depend on afterthought,
matanoia, in order to mend mistakes which forethought would
have avoided. But 'an afterthought' may very easily be *a changed
thought*. In the light of the consequences, in the light of a new
appreciation of the circumstances, in the light of new knowledge
and new awareness a man's second thoughts may be very different from his first thoughts; and it is from this that *metanoia*
comes to mean 'repentance'. If we begin from here, we can see
that in all true repentance there must be four different elements.

(i)   There must be the realization that one's actions were
wrong. A man must come to realize that he was mistaken and
on the wrong way.

(ii)   There must be sorrow for his error, for his wrong-doing,
for his sin.

(iii)   There must come a changed attitude to life, to conduct
and to action as a whole. Repentance does not simply mean that
a man is sorry for the consequences of the thing which he did,

or the course of action which he has taken. It means that he has come to see the wrongness of the whole attitude of mind, the whole view of life, which made him act as he did. To take an example, a man may live loosely and immorally in the sphere of sexual relationships; he may thereby injure his body and contract some disease. Repentance does not mean simply being sorry that this consequence of his own immorality has come upon him; it means the coming of the awareness that his whole view of life, his whole attitude to personal relationships, was wrong, and the awakening of bitter sorrow in his heart that he ever was the kind of man he was, and that he ever had the attitude to life he had. The godly sorrow of repentance must never be confused with sorrow for the consequences of a deed, although it is true that the sudden realization of the consequences may awaken true repentance in a man's heart.

(iv) There must follow a change of action to fit the change of mind. A change of life must accompany the change of heart. A man must bring forth fruits meet for repentance. This is well shown by another Greek word which very commonly accompanies *metanoia* and *metanoein*. This is the word *epistrephein*, which means 'to turn'. When the people of Lydda heard Peter, they *turned* to the Lord (Acts 9.35). In Antioch a great number believed and *turned* to the Lord (Acts 11.21). It is Paul's appeal to the people of Lystra that they should *turn* from earthly vanities to the living God (Acts 14.15). The Gentiles who have *turned* to God are to be admitted into the Church without more ado (Acts 15.19). Paul's commission is to *turn* men from darkness to light (Acts 26.18). Paul tells Agrippa how he preached that men should *repent* and *turn* to God (Acts 26.20).

The picture is that a man is facing in one direction—away from God—and in repentance he changes his direction—towards God. Repentance means a turning round and a facing in the opposite direction. There is a strange and cryptic saying of Jesus reported in the apocryphal *Acts of Peter*:

> Except ye make the right hand as the left hand, and the left hand as the right hand, and that which is upwards as that which is downwards, that which is before as that which is behind, ye shall not know the Kingdom of God.

When does the right become the left, the left the right, and that which is before that which is behind? *Obviously when a man turns round.* When does that which is upwards become as that which is downwards? When a man is, so to speak, stood on his head, that is, when he begins to see the world the other way round, when his values are reversed, when the things he thought important become unimportant, and when the things he disregarded become the most important things in life. Repentance means the reversal of the direction of life in order to face God.

All these four elements must be present, or repentance is unreal. Without the realization of sin, repentance cannot even begin. Saul Kane discovers 'the harm I've done by being me'. But a man may be quite unaware of the error of his ways, quite blind to the ugliness of his life, quite insensitive to the grief and the pain which he is causing to other people. Or he may be well aware that he is doing wrong, but not be in the least sorry for it. He may in fact glory and take a pride in his ability to do as he likes, to get his own way, to break the laws of honesty and honour. Or he may cease from his wrong-doing, but his attitude to it may be in no way changed. He may cease simply from fear of the consequences, simply from lack of opportunity, and, if a way came to him whereby he might continue in his wrongdoing and escape the consequences or be able to hide it in secrecy, he would certainly take it. His view of life has in no way altered. Or he may be really sorry for his sin; his attitude to life may be truly altered; but at the same time his sin may have such a grip and a power over him that he cannot leave it. He may be powerless to break the self-forged chains which bind him.

And now we come to the final step in the matter. A man cannot take any of the steps of repentance *without the help of Jesus Christ.* A man cannot realize his own sin and the ugliness of his own life, until he sees goodness and compares himself with it. He must see his secret or open sins in the light of Jesus Christ's pure countenance. When a man sets his own life in the light of the life of the Lord of all good life, then he realizes his sin. A man cannot be truly sorry for sin until he sees the whole consequences of sin. In the Cross of Christ he is enabled to see what sin can do; he is enabled to see that sin can take the loveliest life the world ever saw and smash and break it on a cross. The cross shows every man the terrible destructive power of sin. A man cannot break the chains that bind him, he cannot turn his godly sorrow into an effective change of life, without the enabling power of Jesus Christ. It is only with and through Jesus Christ that he can make the change which repentance demands. Repentance is begun, continued and ended in Jesus Christ.

So, then, Jesus came with the imperative *Repent!* It was a word which men would immediately recognize. It was an ancient cry. It was with that summons that John the Baptizer had come (Mark 1.4; Matt. 3.2; Luke 3.3.). It was a summons which had rung for ever through the teaching of the prophets. Jesus the prophet came to summon men to repentance; but he did more— he came to make the essential repentance possible, and only he could do that.

6

THE KINGDOM OF GOD

'Repent,' said Jesus, 'for the kingdom of heaven it at hand' (Matt. 4.17). We have looked at the imperative of Jesus— 'Repent!' Now we must look at the indicative of Jesus—'The kingdom of heaven is at hand.'

We must begin by noting one minor point. The Gospels use two phrases, the Kingdom of God and the Kingdom of Heaven— and they mean exactly the same. The approximate figures for the usage of the two phrases in the Gospels are that Matthew speaks about the Kingdom of Heaven thirty times and of the Kingdom of God only three times: Mark and Luke speak about the Kingdom of God sixteen and thirty-two times respectively and do not use the phrase the Kingdom of Heaven at all. We may see the equivalence of the two phrases by comparing Matt. 19.23, Mark 10.23 and Luke 18.24. Matthew gives the saying of Jesus in the form: 'It will be hard for a rich man to enter the kingdom of heaven.' Mark and Luke give it in the form: 'How hard it will be for those who have riches to enter the kingdom of God.' Matthew himself in the very next verse (19.24) goes on to say: 'It is easier for a camel to go through the eye of a needle than for a rich man to enter the kingdom of God.' Clearly the two expressions are interchangeable.

The reason for the two forms is this. The name of God was so holy that no devout Jew would lightly take it on his lips. Such was his reverence for the sacred name that he always sought for some fitting way to avoid speaking it. One of the simplest ways to avoid the use of the name of God was to speak of heaven instead. Matthew is the most Jewish of all the Gospel writers. He therefore hesitates in reverence to use the name of God, and so, instead of speaking about the Kingdom of God, he habitually speaks about the Kingdom of Heaven.

A second and most important point to be noted is the meaning of the word 'Kingdom'. As it is commonly used in modern speech, a kingdom is a territory, an area of land. The Kingdom of Britain is the territory which belongs to Britain. But that is not what the word means in the New Testament. In the New Testament the Kingdom of God is not the area or territory which belongs to God; it is the sovereignty, the lordship, the rule and the reign of God. The Kingdom of God is not the territory over which God reigns as an earthly king reigns; it is the sovereignty of God, a state and condition of things in which God rules and reigns supreme.

The idea of the Kingdom of God, the sovereignty of God, was a conception which was central and basic to the message of Jesus. He emerged upon men with the message that the Kingdom was at hand (Matt. 4.17; Mark 1.15). To preach the Kingdom was an obligation that was laid upon him (Luke 4.43). It was with the message of the Kingdom that he went through the towns and the villages of Galilee (Luke 8.1). The announcement of the Kingdom was the central element in the teaching of Jesus.

The expression itself was familiar to Jewish ears. The Jewish rabbis and teachers drew a distinction and a contrast between the 'yoke of heavenly sovereignty' and 'the ungodly sovereignty' or 'the yoke of flesh and blood'. They held that God's sovereignty upon earth began with Abraham. 'Before our father Abraham came into the world,' they said, 'God was, as it were, only the King of heaven; but when Abraham came, Abraham made him to be King over heaven and earth.' To the rabbis the sovereignty of God was intimately connected with obedience to the law. The Gentile who became a proselyte and who submitted himself and his life to the law was said to 'take upon himself the sovereignty of heaven'. Every synagogue service began—and still begins—with the recital of the *Shema:* 'Hear, O Israel, The Lord our God is one Lord; and you shalt love the Lord your God with all your heart, and with all your soul, and with all your might' (Deut. 6.4-10); and every time a man shared in the recital of that essential creed of Israel he was said to take upon himself again the sovereignty of the yoke of God.

This sovereignty of God reigned within Israel, but the time was to come when it would reign and rule over all the people of the earth, and when all peoples would submit themselves to it, and when it would be as wide as the world. Since God, being God, is already the Lord of all the earth, although there are so many who have not yet accepted his lordship, the Jewish teachers spoke not so much of the *coming* of the sovereignty of God, as of the *manifestation* or the *appearing* of the sovereignty of God. They looked forward to the day, not when that sovereignty would begin, for it already existed, but when it would be aceepted by all, and so manifested throughout the whole earth.

This idea of the sovereignty of God was conceivable in two different ways. There was the idea of popular Jewish thought. According to this idea, all time may be divided into two ages— this present age, and the age to come. This present age is wholly evil, beyond help and beyond hope and beyond cure, wholly give over to evil. The age to come is wholly good, the age in which the sovereignty of God will be a reality. No human means can turn the one age into the other; that must be done by the direct action of God and the direct breaking in of God into time and into this world. That will happen on the Day of the Lord, which will be the end of one age and the beginning of another. It will come with suddenness and unexpectedness; it will be a time of cosmic upheaval and of the shattering of the entire scheme of things as they are; it will be a time of terror and of judgment in which the world as it is will be destroyed; and then out of the chaos and the travail and the birthpangs will arise the new age in which God is supreme. But there was also another idea which obtained in at least some circles of rabbinic thought. It looked on the coming of the sovereignty of God as a slow process, in which more and more universally men submitted themselves to the yoke of the law, until in the end the sovereignty of God was accepted and admitted by all. The way to it might be different, but Jewish thought never for one moment abandoned the conception that in the end the sovereignty of God would be supreme.

When we turn to the teaching of Jesus about the Kingdom, as it is reported to us in the Gospels, we find a wealth of material, pointing apparently in more than one direction and leading apparently to more than one conclusion. It will, therefore, be better to set down the material as it comes, and so try to allow a pattern to emerge from it, than to begin with a preconceived pattern and to try to fit the material to it.

In the Gospels the Kingdom is often spoken of as something which has come, something which has not emerged from history but which has invaded time out of eternity, something which has not arisen on earth but which has descended from heaven, something which is in no sense an achievement or attainment of man but which is entirely the gift and the work of God.

When Jesus healed the demon-possessed man, he said: 'If it is by the finger of God that I cast out demons, then the Kingdom of God has come upon you' (Luke 11.20; Matt. 12.28). It is God's good pleasure to give Jesus' men the Kingdom (Luke 12.32). The Kingdom is *preached* (Matt. 4.23; 9.35; 24.14; Luke 9.2). The Kingdom is *proclaimed* (Luke 9.60). The good news of the Kingdom is *announced* (Luke 8.1). The Kingdom may be *received* (Mark 10.15; Luke 18.17). The Kingdom may be *entered* (Matt. 5.20; 18.3; 19.23; Mark 10.23-25; Luke 18.24f.). A man may *be not far from* the Kingdom (Mark 12.34). Only a reality which is already given and already present can be spoken of in such terms.

Further, this coming of the Kingdom, this entry of the Kingdom into the present world, is something entirely new, something literally epoch-making. Great as John the Baptizer is, the man who is least in the Kingdom is greater than he (Luke 7.28). Up to the time of John the law and the prophets existed—and none will question the greatness of either—but since John the Kingdom of God is preached (Luke 16.16). The Kingdom is something which by its emergence has put everything that went before it out of date. In the giving of the Kingdom God has done a new thing for men.

It is nevertheless also true that the Kingdom is of long and ancient standing. Abraham and Isaac and Jacob and all the prophets are in the Kingdom of God (Luke 13.28: Matt. 8.11). Even in their day it was possible for a man to enter the Kingdom. In this sense the Kingdom is no new thing but goes back to the beginning of man's search for and discovery of God.

In spite of all this it is nonetheless true that the Kingdom has still to come, that it is still in some sense in the future. Joseph of Arimathaea was waiting for the Kingdom (Mark 15.43; Luke 23.51). It is the promise of Jesus that the Kingdom will come with power within the lifetime of some of those who were actually listening to him (Mark 9.1; Matt. 16.28; Luke 9.27). It is the hope and the faith of Jesus that he will drink the cup new in his Father's Kingdom (Mark 14.25; Matt. 26.29). The coming of the Kingdom is an event for which Jesus taught his people to pray (Matt. 6.10; Luke 11.2), and men do not pray for that which they already possess.

And yet it still remains true that the Kingdom is a present reality. The Kingdom is within you, or among you (*entos humōn*) (Luke 17.21). It is necessary to find some explanation of the meaning of the Kingdom which will cover the fact that the Kingdom can be—and is—past, present and future at one and the same time, that the Kingdom goes back to the patriarchs and the prophets, and yet at the same time with the coming of Jesus is so near that men can feel the breath of it upon them (Matt. 4.17; 10.7; 12.28; Mark 1.15.; Luke 10.9,11; 11.20).

We have already seen that the Kingdom is often spoken of as the work and the gift of God, as that which is given, as that which has come by the action of God to men. But in the Gospels there is another and equally strong line of thought about the Kingdom which relates the Kingdom to the most intense and strenuous effort of men.

Men are bidden to *seek* the Kingdom (Matt. 6.33; Luke 12.31). The word is *zētein*, and it has been well translated: 'Make the Kingdom the object of all your endeavour.' Men are said to *press* into the Kingdom (Matt. 11.12; Luke 16.16). The word is *biazesthai*, and it is the word used of attackers storming a city. Men must storm their way into the Kingdom. 'The Kingdom,' as Denney said, 'is not for the well-meaning but for the desperate.' To enter the Kingdom is *worth any sacrifice*. It is better surgically to cut off any member of the body which would hinder a man from entering the Kingdom than to preserve the body whole and to be shut out of the Kingdom (Matt. 5.29f.; Mark 9.43-48).

There are at least two passages in which by implication the Kingdom is equated with *life* itself. If we compare Mark 9.43, 45,47, we shall see that in the first two verses it is *life* that is spoken of, and in the third it is the *Kingdom* that is spoken of, and the meaning is the same. In the story of the rich young ruler the request of the young man is for guidance as to how he is to find *eternal life* (Matt. 19.16; Mark 10.17; Luke 18.18); and, when he has made his tragic departure, the word of Jesus deals with how difficult it is for a rich man to enter the *Kingdom of*

God (Matt. 19.23; Mark 10.23; Luke 18.24). By implication the Kingdom is nothing less than heaven, and nothing less than life.

Even if we regard the Kingdom as entirely given, as entirely the gift of God, it still remains true that the teaching of Jesus lays down certain very definite conditions regarding entry to the Kingdom. No man can enter the Kingdom without *the child-like spirit* (Matt. 18.1). No man can enter the Kingdom without *the forgiving spirit* (Matt. 18.23-35). No man can enter the Kingdom without *a certain attitude to his fellow-men* (Matt. 25.31-46). If his attitude to men is an insensitive unawareness of the needs and the sorrows of others, he is shut out from the Kingdom. If a man would enter the Kingdom, his life must be a demonstration of love, *agapē*, in action. No man can enter the Kingdom without *a certain standard of righteousness*. The Christian standard of righteousness must exceed the righteousness of the scribes and Pharisees, or there is no entry to the Kingdom (Matt. 5.20). The teaching of Jesus uncompromisingly lays down the conditions of entry into the Kingdom.

As there are certain conditions of entry to the Kingdom, so there are certain hindrances to entry into it. *Riches* are a grave hindrance to entry to the Kingdom; it is very hard for a rich man to enter the Kingdom of God (Matt. 19.23f.; Mark 10.23-25; Luke 18.24f.). Riches encourage a false independence in a man, making him feel that he can buy his way into, or buy his way out of, anything. When a man is rich, he has so big a stake in this earth that it is very difficult for him to see beyond it, or to contemplate leaving it. Riches are not a sin, but they are a very grave danger and threat to a man's entry to the Kingdom. *The inability to make a clear-cut decision* is a hindrance to entry to the Kingdom. If a man puts his hand to the plough, and looks back, he is not fit for entry to the Kingdom (Luke 9.61f.). There are things in life which conspire to keep a man out of the Kingdom.

There is a clear *element of judgment* in the Kingdom. The Kingdom involves a separation and a division between men. This is notably shown in the parables of the tares and of the drag-net (Matt. 13.24-30, 37-43, 47-50). Parable after parable involves a judgment on a man based on how he did or did not accept the opportunities and perform the duties of life. *The invitation to enter the Kingdom can be refused,* just as a man may foolishly and discourteously refuse an invitation to be the guest at a feast (Matt. 22.1-14; Luke 14.15-24). *The opportunity to enter the Kingdom can be lost,* just as the foolish bridesmaids lost their opportunity to share in the joy of the wedding festivities (Matt. 25.1-13). *The privilege of entering the Kingdom may be taken away,* as Jesus warned those who had consistently spurned the messengers of God, and those whose reaction to himself was without faith and without love (Matt. 21.43; Matt. 8.11; Luke 13.28).

There is no doubt that, even if the Kingdom is given independently of the action of men, a man by his own actions and reactions has much to do with his entry to it, or with his failure to enter it.

Having assembled our material we have now to ask if there is any general principle which emerges from it, and if there is any pattern into which all the varied ideas of the Kingdom can be fitted. We have the paradox that the Kingdom is at once past, present and future. It is something into which the prophets and the patriarchs entered; it is something which is here now within or among men; and it is something for which Jesus taught his disciples still to pray. We have the paradox that the Kingdom is something which is given, and which is the direct result of the personal action of God, and that yet at the same time it is something which is very much dependent on the action and the reaction of men.

The outstanding difficulty which confronts us in any study of the Kingdom is the fact that nowhere in the teaching of Jesus is the Kingdom defined. It is continuously illustrated by parable after parable. Its invitations, its demands, its paramount importance are consistently stressed. The danger and the terrible consequences of failure to enter it are again and again underlined. But no concise definition of it ever appears. Since that is so, we must try to deduce our own definition of it .

In the Lord's Prayer two petitions appear side by side (Matt. 6.10):

Thy kingdom come,
Thy will be done, on earth as it is in heaven.

By far the commonest feature of Hebrew style is *parallelism*. The repetition of a statement in a parallel form is a characteristic of Jewish poetical style. In this repetition the second of the two parallel statements repeats, amplifies or explains the first. Almost any verse of the Psalms will illustrate this method of writing in action.

The Lord of hosts is with us;
The God of Jacob is our refuge (Ps. 46.7).

He makes me lie down in green pastures,
He leads me beside still waters (Ps. 23.2).

The earth is the Lord's and the fulness thereof,
The world and those who dwell therein (Ps. 24.1).

The Lord is your keeper;
The Lord is your shade
On your right hand (Ps. 121.5).

In each case the parallel repeats the first statement in such a way as to amplify or to explain it. Let us again set down the two parallel phrases in the Lord's Prayer:

Thy kingdom come,
Thy will be done, on earth as it is in heaven (Matt. 6.10).

Now let us apply the principle of parallelism to these two phrases; let us assume that the second amplifies and explains the first. We then arrive at this definition of the Kingdom: *The Kingdom is a state of things on earth in which God's will is as perfectly done as it is in heaven*. If this definition is accepted, the pattern begins to fall into place.

(i) It is a natural definition of the Kingdom. To be a citizen of any kingdom is to accept and to obey its laws; therefore, to be a citizen of the Kingdom of God must be to accept and to obey the laws of God. If the Kingdom of God means the sovereignty of God, then no man can be within that Kingdom unless he submits himself to the lordship of God in perfect obedience to the will of God.

(ii)   This conception of the Kingdom individualizes the Kingdom. Membership of the Kingdom now becomes a matter between each man and God, and involves the personal acceptance by each man of the will of God. The Kingdom becomes not a vague generality but a personal issue between a man and God. To enter the Kingdom means personally to accept the will of God. It must be clearly realized that, although this conception of the Kingdom individualizes the Kingdom, it does not turn the Kingdom into a selfish thing; for to accept the will of God is not only to be in a certain relationship to God, it is very definitely also to be in a certain relationship to men. No man can be oblivious to the claims of his fellow-men upon him and at the same time accept the will of God.

(iii)   This conception of the Kingdom explains how the Kingdom can be at one and the same time past, present and future. Any men who in any age and generation accepted the will of God was within the Kingdom. Any man who today accepts the will of God is within the Kingdom. But two things are clear. The world is still very far from a condition in which all men accept the will of God; and the individual man is still not in a condition in which he consistently, constantly and uninterruptedly accepts the will of God. For most men the acceptance of the will of God is still spasmodic. The rebellion of the human heart, the resentment of the human spirit, and the instinctive independence of the human will are still far from being eradicated in us. Therefore, the full consummation of the Kingdom is still in the future, and must still be an object of man's prayers and man's endeavours.

(iv)   This conception of the Kingdom enables us to understand the place of Jesus in the Kingdom. Through him the Kingdom had come and was to come. In him the new thing had entered into life and into the world so that the time which followed his coming was different from the time which preceded it. This is true for three reasons.

(a)   In Jesus the Kingdom was embodied. He alone of all who had ever lived, or ever would live, perfectly and completely fulfilled the will of God. The very essence of his life is obedience to the will of God. At the beginning he met the tempter with a quotation from the word of God, thereby opposing the invitation to take the wrong way by setting over against it the will of God. In the end in Gethsemane he won his final battle before the Cross by saying: 'Thy will be done' (Matt. 26.36-46; Mark 14.32-42; Luke 22.39-46). All through his earthly life he had these times of retirement when he sought for himself the will of God. The Fourth Gospel depicts Jesus as saying: 'My food is to do the will of him who sent me, and to accomplish his work' (John 4.34). The whole picture of Jesus in the Gospels is the picture of one who began, continued and ended his life in complete and chosen obedience to the will of God. That is why it can be said that in and with Jesus the Kingdom came. He was the perfect embodiment and the perfect demonstration of the meaning of the Kingdom.

(b) The very fact that he rendered to God this complete obedience meant that through him there were unleashed in the world powers with which no other person could ever have been trusted and which no other person could ever possess. His unique obedience brought to him a unique power. If any ordinary person were to be entrusted with any kind of miraculous power, the certainty is that he would do with it far more damage than good. It was because of Jesus' perfect obedience that he came to possess his special power.

(c) Not only does Jesus within his own person demonstrate the Kingdom; he also enables others to enter into it. He removes the barrier between God and men. He cancels the power of past sin and by his Spirit and his presence enables men to overcome present sin. He thereby enables men also to accept and to obey the will of God, and so to enter the Kingdom of God.

It remains only to test out this conception of the Kingdom on typical Gospel passages. When we are bidden to seek the Kingdom (Matt. 6.33; Luke 12.31), it means that we are bidden all through life to make the acceptance of the will of God the object of all our endeavour, and then life will bring all its blessedness to us. When we are bidden to cut away anything that will hinder entry to the Kingdom (Mark 9.43-48), or when the Kingdom is likened to a man who finds some precious thing and sells his all to buy it (Matt. 13.44-46), it means that it is worth any sacrifice to accept and to do the will of God. When the childlike spirit is said to be a necessity of entry to the Kingdom (Matt.

18.1), it means that we must bring to God the obedience which a child owes and brings to his parents. When the forgiving spirit is said to be a condition of entry to the Kingdom (Matt. 18.23-35), and when a certain attitude to men is said to be necessary for entry to the Kingdom (Matt. 25.31-46), it means that we must forgive as God forgives and treat men as God treats men. When it is said that the Kingdom belongs to the poor in spirit (Matt. 5.3), it means that, when a man realizes his own utter helplessness and worthlessness and inadequacy, and submits his ignorance to God's wisdom, his weakness to God's power, his sin to God's mercy, then he enters the Kingdom of God.

To do the will of God and to be in the Kingdom of God are one and the same thing. Because Jesus did that, he is the embodiment of the Kingdom and in him the Kingdom came. Because he enables others to do that, he is the gateway to the Kingdom. Because the world as yet is very far from making this perfect submission to the will of God, the Kingdom has still to come in all its fulness; but in the end the plan and purpose of God will be realized in a state and condition of things in which his will is as perfectly done on earth and among mankind as it is in heaven and in Jesus Christ, for that is the Kingdom.

7

THE POINT OF ATTACK

A LEADER must not only choose the area in which he will launch his campaign; he must also choose the point within the area at which he will direct his initial attack. The problem which faced Jesus was the problem which faces every man with a message—the problem of communication. Already he had chosen Galilee as the area of his initial campaign. At what point within Galilee was he to make his beginning?

If today a man was convinced that he had a message from God, in what place would he most naturally seek to begin to deliver that message? Quite certainly such a man with such a message would begin in the Church. He would certainly feel that there his message would receive an interested and receptive audience.

In Palestine in the time of Jesus there were two places which correspond to the modern Church. There was the Temple. But the Temple was not the place in which Jesus could begin. In the whole land there was only one Temple, the Temple in Jerusalem. The one reason for the existence of the Temple was the offering of sacrifice. In the Temple there was no preaching and no instruction. There was sacrifice; there was prayer; there was music; and on certain occasions there was the reading of Scripture; but in the ritual and liturgy and services of the Temple there was no place for preaching and instruction, and no opportunity for the delivery of a message from God by word of mouth.

There was the synagogue. The case of the synagogue was quite different. There were synagogues in every town and village; the law was that, wherever there were ten Jewish families, a synagogue must be built. Sacrifice was no part of the synagogue worship. The synagogue was primarily and essentially a teaching institution. The synagogues have been described as 'the popular religious universities of their day'. If a man had a message from God for the people, the synagogue was the place in which to deliver it.

Further, the order of service in the synagogue was such as to give the opportunity desired. The synagogue service consisted of three parts. It began with a time of prayer. It centred in a time for the reading of Scripture in which both the law and the prophets were read, with members of the congregation sharing in the reading. It was for this reading of Scripture that the synagogue really existed. It went on to a time of preaching and teaching. In the synagogue there was no one person to preach the sermon, give the address, or expound the teaching. The ruler or president of the synagogue was neither teacher or preacher; he was an administrative official whose business it was to see that the business of the synagogue was carried out with efficiency and the services with decency and order and reverence. It was the custom that any distinguished person present, anyone with a message, was invited to give his message and to address the congregation. Here, indeed, was the opportunity for any man with a message from God to give it. In every town and village where there were Jews he would find a synagogue, and in the synagogue service he would find an open opportunity to deliver his message.

Here, then, was the place for Jesus to begin. Here, at least at the beginning of his ministry, before he was branded as rebel and heretic, he would find a ready-made congregation and an opportunity to speak to them. So we find him in the synagogue in Capernaum (Mark 1.21). We find him going round Galilee teaching in the synagogues wherever he went (Matt. 4.23; 9.35; 12.9; Mark 1.39; 3.1; Luke 4.15; 4.44; 6.6; 13.10). It always had been, and still was, his custom to go into the synagogue on the Sabbath day (Luke 4.16). It was therefore in the synagogue that Jesus deliberately began to deliver his message.

What, then, was the message which Jesus brought to the congregations of the synagogues up and down Galilee? Luke gives us an account of Jesus' visit to the synagogue at Nazareth (Luke 4.16-30). As we have already seen, in the synagogue the congregation shared in the reading of Scripture. In Nazareth Jesus received the duty of reading the lesson from the prophets. It was from Isa. 61:

The Spirit of the Lord is upon me,
because he has anointed me to preach good news to the poor.
He has sent me to proclaim release to the captives
and recovering of sight to the blind,
to set at liberty those who are oppressed,
to proclaim the acceptable year of the Lord.

Clearly in that passage Jesus saw the picture of himself. 'To-day,' he said, 'this scripture has been fulfilled in your hearing' (Luke 4.21). This is the essence of the message of Jesus, and, if that be so, we can at once tell certain things which he must have felt and believed about himself and about his task and about the message which he came to bring to men.

He regarded himself as under obedience and as under orders. He regarded himself as *sent* by God. It was at God's command that he had come, and it was the orders of God that he was carrying out. He was the envoy and apostle of God, as indeed the writer of the Letter to the Hebrews was later to call him (Heb. 3.1).

He regarded himself as equipped with the power of the Spirit. He regarded himself as *empowered* by God. He was who he was, he did what he did, he spoke as he spoke, because the Spirit was on him.

He regarded himself as the *fulfilment* of all that the prophets had said and dreamed. In him the visions of the prophets, the hopes of men, and the promises of God came true. As Paul was later to say: 'All the promises of God find their Yes in him' (II Cor. 1.20). He did not come to destroy the past, but to fulfil the past. He is the one for whom men throughout the centuries have been waiting.

He regarded himself as the messenger of *mercy*. There is a curious deliberate finality in the way in which Luke tells how Jesus read this passage. He read this great promise of the mercy of God, and then *he closed the book* (Luke 4.20). If that is so, then Jesus actually stopped in the middle of a verse as the verses are arranged in the English version of Isaiah. He stopped half-way through Isa. 61.2. And what follows? At what does Jesus stop? He stops at the words 'to proclaim . . . *the day of vengeance of our God.*' That part of the prophecy Jesus did not read. We can only think that he stopped there because he did not regard that at his task; it was mercy, not vengeance, that he came to offer men; it was love, not wrath. He is above and beyond all else the messenger of mercy.

The mercy which Jesus promised and brought was of *the most practical kind*. It was good news for the poor; it was liberty to the captives; it was sight to the blind; it was freedom for the oppressed; it was the mercy and the grace of God for which all had been waiting.

Here is the great characteristic of the message which Jesus brought. It was a promise, and not a threat. It was the offer of the mercy and the grace and the love of God, and not the threat of the wrath and the vengeance and the anger of God. He came above all to bring gifts to men.

Already in Nazareth the shadow of things to come fell across the path of Jesus. So far from welcoming his message, the people of Nazareth resented it. Did they not know his parents? Were his brothers and sisters not still living in the town? Had he not himself been the village carpenter before he left home? What right had he to speak like that? (Matt. 13.55-57; Mark 6.3-6; Luke 4.22-30.) Many motives were to combine to lead to the crucifying of Jesus. At the very beginning he met the simplest and the most human of them all—the inveterate prejudice of his fellow-men against the man who dares to be different and who fails to conform to the conventions of his environment. Men hate to be disturbed, especially by one of themselves.

8

CHOOSING HIS MEN

A LEADER may map out his campaign with the greatest care; he may choose his sphere of operations, his time and place of attack with the greatest skill and insight; but ultimately he is dependent on his men, and especially on his staff. 'One man,' said Field Marshal Montgomery, 'can lose me a battle.' Unless the leader has men on whom he can rely to accept his orders and to carry out his plans, all his own wisdom and foresight can go for nothing.

Douglas Blatherwick in *A Layman Speaks* tells how in the Champness Hall in Rochdale there was a concert by the Hallé Orchestra under Sir John Barbirolli. The hall was crowded to capacity. As the crowd was leaving the hall a man said to the minister: 'When are you going to have this place full on a Sunday evening?' The minister answered: 'I shall have this place full on a Sunday evening when, like Sir John Barbirolli, I have under me eighty trained and disciplined men.' Anyone leading a campaign must have a staff through whom he can act. And that was true of Jesus. So the time came when Jesus chose the men who were to be his twelve apostles. There were two great reasons why he chose them.

(i) Jesus chose his men *because his work had to go on*. Jesus never had any doubt that for himself there was a cross at the end of the road; he knew that in the end he must die. Already in Nazareth an attempt had been made on his life. There they had hustled him to the hilltop in order to hurl him down, but he had escaped from their hands (Luke 4.29). If his work was to go on, he had to gather round him an inner circle of men whom he could train to know him, to understand him at least in part, and to love him, who would come to know his purpose and his task, and who would carry it on when he had to leave the world in the body. For him his men had to be the living books on which he imprinted his message, the living instruments through whom his purposes could be carried out. In modern times, if a man wished to perpetuate his message, he might write it in a book, and so commit it to posterity, but in the days of Jesus there was no such thing as a printed book. Robertson Smith writes of the eastern ideal in those days: 'The ideal of instruction is oral teaching, and the worthiest shrine of truths that must not die is the memory and heart of the faithful disciple.' Jesus had to have his own men, if his work was to go on.

(ii)   He chose them *because his work must go out*. In his days in the flesh Jesus was under all the limitations of space and time. His presence could be in only one place at a time; his voice could reach only a limited number of people. In that ancient world there were no means of mass communication, such as print and newspapers and wireless now provide. If any message had to be taken to men, it had to be taken to them personally. So Jesus had to have men to go where he could not go, and to speak where he could not speak.

In his book *Then and Now* Dr John Foster tells how an enquirer from Hinduism came to an Indian bishop seeking baptism. The man had read the New Testament without help and guidance, entirely by himself, and he had seen the meaning of it. The picture of Jesus in the Gospels fascinated him; and the Cross moved him to the depths of his being.

> Then he read on . . . and felt he had entered into a new world. In the Gospels it was Jesus, his works and his suffering. In the Acts. . . . what the disciples did and thought and taught had taken the place that Christ had occupied. The Church continued where Jesus left off at his death. 'Therefore,' said this man to me, 'I must belong to the Church that carries on the life of Christ.'

Jesus needed his men so that through them his work might go on and might go out. They were to be in a very real sense his body, so that in them and through them he might continue his work and extend it in time to all men.

There are three accounts of the choosing of the twelve—Mark 3.13-19; Matt. 10.1-4; Luke 6.13-16. Each of these accounts has its own contribution to make to our understanding of the purpose of Jesus in choosing the twelve.

(i)   Jesus offered the twelve an *invitation*. As Mark has it: 'He *called* to him those whom he desired' (Mark 3.13). As Luke has it: 'He *called* his disciples' (Luke 6.13). The word for 'to call' is different in the two Gospels. In Mark it is *proskaleisthai,* which means rather 'to invite', and in Luke it is *prosphōnein,* which means rather 'to summon'. So, then, Jesus began with two things. He began with an *invitation.* An invitation is something which can be accepted or refused at the decision of him who receives it. It was volunteers, not conscripts, whom Jesus sought as his men. He began with a *challenge.* Jesus invited men neither to ease or to safety; he invited them neither to honour or to prestige; he invited them neither to financial gain or material advancement. There was little to be gained by attaching themselves to a penniless Galilaean wanderer, who was clearly on the way to a head-on clash with the religious authorites of the day. It was a challenge to leave all, to take up a cross, and to follow him. Jesus always challenged, and never bribed, men into allegiance to himself.

(ii) The invitation was in fact a *selection.* 'Jesus called his disciples, and chose from them twelve' (Luke 6.13). The word is *eklegesthai,* and it implies deliberate choice and selection. As John was later to put it, Jesus was in effect saying: 'You did not choose me, but I chose you' (John 15.19). Out of the crowds who were loosely attached to him these men were chosen to be indissolubly bound to him, to be his staff, his shock troops, his righthand men.

(iii) The invitation and the selection were in fact *an appointment* to a task and office. 'He appointed (*poiein*) twelve' (Mark 3.14). This was a setting apart for special service, an appointment for a special place in the plan and the purpose of God.

(iv) The invitation and selection were for certain great purposes. Jesus chose his men that *they should be with him* (Mark 3.14). They were to be with him for two reasons. They were to be with him *for his own sake.* Jesus, too, needed friends. 'A friend,' said Aristotle in a great phrase, 'is another self.' Jesus needed those to whom he could open his heart and reveal his mind. A man can bear many things in life, but the hardest of all things to bear is loneliness; a man can dispense with many things in life, but he cannot dispense with friendship. 'No longer,' Jesus was to say, 'do I call you servants ... but I have called you friends' (John 15.15). It may well be said that the greatest of all Christian titles is 'the friend of Jesus'.

They were to be with him *for their sakes*. It is the simple and the obvious truth that no man can bring Jesus to others until he knows him himself. The Christian life must always be a two-way process, a coming in to Jesus and a going out to men. The Christian must live constantly *with* Christ, if he is to live *for* Christ among men.

(v) The object of this companying with Jesus can best of all be seen in one of the great names of the Christian—the name *disciple*. The *disciple* is in Greek the *mathētēs*, the learner. Confronted with the unsearchable riches of Christ (Eph. 3.8), the Christian must always be learning more and more about his Lord and about the way of Jesus. One of the greatest threats to a real Christian life is what might be called static Christianity. The great fact of sanctification must never be forgotten. In Greek sanctification is *hagiasmos*; Greek nouns which end in *-asmos* regularly denote and describe a process, and *hagiasmos*, sanctification, is *the road to holiness*. The Christian is the disciple, the learner, penetrating ever more deeply into the wonder of Jesus, because he lives with him.

(vi) But the object of this companying with Jesus is seen just as much in another great title for the twelve; they were the *apostles*. The word apostle means 'one who is sent out'. The kindred word *apostolē* can mean a naval squadron, and the word itself can mean an ambassador. 'He appointed twelve to be with him, and *to be sent out* to preach' (Mark 3.14). Both Matthew and Luke actually call the twelve the apostles (Matt. 10.2; Luke 6.13). The twelve were called to be with Christ that they might be sent out to be his heralds, his envoys and his ambassadors to men.

(vii) They were sent out with two main functions. They were sent out *to preach* and *to heal* (Mark 3.14f.; Matt. 10.7f.). The normal New Testament word for 'to preach' is *kērussein*, which is the verb of the noun *kērux*, which means 'a herald'. The twelve were to be the heralds of the King, bringing to men the announcement of the arrival of the King, and the proclamation of the message of the King. In their healing they were to bring to men, not a theoretical exposition, but a practical demonstration of the love of God.

Jesus described the work of his men in a special phrase, and he gave them a special title. He said that he would make them *fishers of men* (Matt. 4.19; Mark 1.17; Luke 5.10). In point of fact many of them were fishermen by trade, and this title is a one-word summary of the kind of men which they must be, and the way in which they must approach their work.

(i)   The very circumstances of a fisherman's life and work compel him to live close to God. Any man who day by day faces the elemental forces of nature and their threats is bound to be aware of God. It is a common saying that there are no atheists among sailors. The very fact that their life was on the waters, amidst the storms and the waves, made them aware of God. Jesus chose to be his men those for whom God was already a very present reality.

(ii)   They were necessarily men of courage. The seaman, perhaps more than any other man, constantly takes his life in his hands. The seaman prayed to whatever gods there be for protection: 'My boat is so small and the sea is so large.' Dr Johnson in one of his sweeping statements once said: 'No man will be a sailor who has contrivance enough to get himself into a jail; for being in a ship is being in a jail, with the chance of being drowned.' The twelve were men to whom taking a risk was part of the day's work. They were men to whom launching out into the deep was a daily experience.

(iii)   They were necessarily men of patience and perseverance. There must be a certain undiscourageability about the man who will be a fisherman. Often he will have to wait long; often all his toil will be for nothing, and he will have to come home empty-handed, prepared to start all over again. The fisherman is already a man who has learned to work and to wait and to go on in face of apparent failure.

(iv)   They were necessarily men of judgment. The fisherman must wisely choose his time, his place, his net, his bait. That too is the problem of the fisher of men. He must be wise enough to choose his time of approach, his method of approach, his way of presenting the offer of Christ to fit each individual case, or he may well lose more men than he will win.

Jesus chose his staff with wisdom. He chose men who had learned the lessons of life not in an academy or in a seminary but in the business of living. He chose men whom life had already moulded for his purposes. He chose them, first to be with him, then to be sent out as his ambassadors to men.

9

THE MIRACLES OF JESUS

W E have already listened to Jesus' opening manifesto in the synagogue in Nazareth (Luke 4.18):

> The Spirit of the Lord is upon me,
> because he has anointed me to preach good news to the poor.
> He has sent me to proclaim release to the captives
> and recovering of sight to the blind,
> to set at liberty those who are oppressed,
> to proclaim the acceptable year of the Lord.

Therein there is outlined a programme of the most practical help, and the determination to accept the task of alleviating the sufferings and the sorrows of men. By that proclamation Jesus was committed to a life, not of words, but of actions. It is clear that he will go out on a campaign in which he will teach as much, and more, by his deeds as by his words.

No one can read the Gospels without being brought face to to face with the miracles of Jesus. The miracles are not extras which may be excised and deleted from the story without injuring its structure and its framework. If we remove the stories of the miracles the whole framework of the Gospel story falls to pieces, and often even the teaching of Jesus is left without an occasion and a context. In the first chapter of Mark there are no fewer than six references to healing. In the synagogue in Capernaum Jesus healed the man with the unclean spirit (Mark 1.23). In the fisherman's cottage he healed Peter's wife's mother (Mark 1.31). In the open air he healed the crowds who came to him at evening time (Mark 1.32-34). He cast out devils from those who were demon-possessed (Mark 1.39). He healed a leper (Mark 1.40-44). The chapter ends with crowds flocking to him for the help and the healing which they were convinced that he could give to them (1.45). Mark opens his story with the picture of Jesus the healer of men.

When we read the Gospel narrative, we come from it with the impression that time and time again Jesus was the centre of a crowd of people eagerly clamouring for healing, and that he was able and willing to heal them all. Again and again we come on passages like this: 'They brought him all the sick, those afflicted with various diseases and pains, demoniacs, epileptics, and paralytics, and he healed them' (Matt. 4.24; cf. Matt. 8.16; 12.15; 14.14; 15.30f.; 19.2; Mark 1.34; 3.10; Luke 4.40; 6.18; 7.21). 'He healed them all' runs like an ever-recurring theme or chorus throughout the gospel narrative.

Very early Matthew lays down what may be called the pattern of the ministry of Jesus: 'He went about all Galilee, teaching in their synagogues and preaching the gospel of the kingdom and healing every disease and every infirmity among the people' (Matt. 4.23; cf. 9.35). Preaching, teaching, healing—that was the threefold pattern of the ministry of Jesus. It was a precisely similar scheme of activity that he laid down for his men when he sent them out on their mission for himself and for the King-dom. He gave them power over unclean spirits and to heal every disease and infirmity; he sent them out to preach that the King-dom was at hand, and to heal the sick, to raise the dead, to cleanse the lepers and to cast out demons (Matt. 10.1,7f.; Mark 6.13; Luke 9.1,6; 10.9). Healing was an inseparable part of the pattern of his work and of the pattern of the work of his apostles.

It was in fact over this very question of healing that there came his head-on clash with the orthodox religious authorities of his day. It was because he healed on the Sabbath day, and thereby broke the Pharisaic Sabbath law, that he was branded as a dangerous and heretical law-breaker, and as one who must be eliminated as quickly as possible. He clashed with the Pharisees over the healing on the Sabbath of the man with the withered hand (Matt. 12.9-14; Mark 3.1-6; Luke 6.6-11), the woman bent for eighteen years with her infirmity (Luke 13.10-17), the man with the dropsy (Luke 14.1-6). It would be impossible to remove Jesus' ministry of healing and to make sense of his whole career.

When we try to understand the miracles of Jesus, we are met with an initial difficulty, the difficulty of defining a miracle. That which would be a miracle in one age or in one society is a commonplace in another. Even fifty years ago people would have regarded it as a miracle to be able to sit in a room and look into a glass-fronted box and see plays being acted, games being played, events happening hundreds and even thousands of miles away. A Viking would have regarded an 80,000-ton ship speeding across the Atlantic as a miracle. A Roman charioteer would have regarded as a miracle a machine which can move through the air faster than sound can travel. Hippocrates or Galen or any other ancient physician would have regarded modern anaesthetics or modern surgical operations on the heart or lungs as a miracle. Julius Caesar or Hannibal, Napoleon or Wellington, would have regarded as a miracle—even if a devilish one—the devastation which one single atom bomb can cause.

We may put this in another way. The conception of *the possible* does not stay steady; it varies from age to age. Everyday we perform as a matter of course actions which previous generations would have regarded as fantastically impossible. We make a railway journey of four hundred and fifty miles at an average speed of sixty miles an hour. We reach a great city, effortlessly move down into the bowels of the earth on a moving staircase, travel through a man-made tunnel, and reach our destination by another moving staircase. We enter an hotel and are whisked up to the sixth floor in an elevator. We shave with an electric razor. We pick up a little instrument and carry on a conversation with some one hundreds of miles away as clearly as if they were in the same room. What would have been an impossibility in one century is a routine action in the next; and what would have been a miracle in one age of history is a commonplace in another. A vivid illustration of this is the simple fact that in the ancient world very few people had ever tasted fresh fish; Epicurus lists it as a luxurious and extravagant delicacy. It was impossible to transport it for any distance and to keep it fresh in transit. And now fish is a staple item of diet.

To define a miracle as something which is impossible is a quite inadequate definition, for who is to define the possible and the impossible in any way which is not relative to his own position in time and in progress?

If we are to understand the miracles of Jesus at all, we must see them against the mental and spiritual climate of the age in which they happened. Since that is so, certain facts about the age of the New Testament have to be taken into account.

That age had a completely different attitude to the miraculous. Modern man is suspicious of the miraculous; he dislikes anything that he cannot explain; and he thinks that he knows so much about the universe and its working that he can say roundly that miracles do not happen. The last thing which he expects is a miracle. On the other hand, the ancient world revelled in the miraculous. It looked for miracles; it expected miracles; and the result was that apparently miraculous events happened. To put it paradoxically and yet truly, the miraculous was a commonplace.

Tacitus and Suetonius are reputable historians, and both are essential sources for the history of the Roman Empire. Both relate an incident from the life of the Roman Emperor Vespasian. In Alexandria there came to Vespasian a man who was blind and who besought him to cure him by touching his eyes with his spittle, and a man who had a diseased hand, who besought him to heal it by touching it with the sole of his foot. At first Vespasian refused to grant the requests, for he had no belief that any cure would follow. Finally he was persuaded. 'He put on a smiling face, and amid an eagerly expectant crowd did what had been asked of him. The hand immediately recovered its power. The blind man saw once again. Both facts are attested to this day, when falsehood can bring no reward, by those who were present on the occasion.'[1] There is every reason to believe that these cures happened, and that they were not uncommon in the ancient world.

In the ancient world the god of healing was Aesculapius. The two great centres of his worship were Rome and Epidaurus. Epidaurus has been called the Lourdes of the ancient world. Sufferers came to these temples, and spent the night there in the darkness. The emblem of Aesculapius is the snake. Accordingly, tame and harmless snakes were let loose in the dormitories; when they touched the people lying there, the people thought that it was the touch of the god, and they were healed.

There was a passage-way at Epidaurus which was covered

[1] Tacitus, *Histories* 4.81; Suetonius, *Vespasian* 7.

with tablets erected by those who had undergone cures. There is a tablet erected by a certain Alketas. 'Though blind he saw the dream vision; the god seemed to come to him and to open his eyes with his fingers, and the first thing he saw was the trees which were in the temple. At daybreak he went away cured.' In the ruins of the temple of Aesculapius at Rome there are many such tablets. There was a certain Julianus who 'was spitting blood and who was given up as hopeless by everyone'. The god sent him a dream oracle. He was to take grains of corn from the altar and for three days he was to eat them with honey. This he did, 'and he was cured, and came and returned thanks publicly before the people.'

One thing is certain. No one goes to the trouble and expense of erecting a marble tablet to commemorate a cure that did not happen. These things happened in the temples of the ancient gods.

We may call it superstition; we may call it a kind of primitive religion; we may call it a childlike faith. The fact is that these people lived in an age which expected miracles. There is a kind of rationalism which kills wonder. When wonder is dead, wonderful things cease to happen. We might well receive more miracles, if we stopped insisting that miracles do not happen, and began expecting them to happen.

This expectancy in the ancient world came from their conviction of the universal nearness of the divine power. Men believed that the world was full of *daimons,* spirits who were intermediaries between the gods and men. Every person, every association of persons, every place had its *daimon.* Samuel Dill describes the mind and soul of that age in *Roman Society from Nero to Marcus Aurelius.* 'With gods in every grove and fountain, and on every mountain summit, with gods breathing in the winds and flashing in the lightning, or the ray of sun and star, heaving in the earthquake or the November storm in the Aegean, watching over every society of men congregated for any purpose, guarding the solitary hunter or traveller in the Alps or the Sahara, what is called miracle became as natural to the heathen as the rising of the sun. In fact, if the gods had not displayed their power in some startling way, their worshippers would have been shocked and forlorn. But the gods did not fail their votaries.

Unquestioning and imperious faith in this kind is always re-
warded, or can always explain its disappointments . . . The divine
power was everywhere, and miracle was in the air.'

The tendency of modern man is to forget God unconsciously
or to eliminate him deliberately, to live in a universe in which he
never thinks of God. In the ancient world men lived in a universe
where they never forgot the mysterious presence of divinity.
Their awareness may have been more closely kin to superstition
than to religion, but none the less things happened, because men
would have been surprised if they did not happen. Men were
open to wonder in a way that is not true of men today.

This belief in the intermingling and the interpenetration of
the human and the divine showed itself in another feature of
life in the ancient world; it showed itself in the belief in demon-
possession. As we can see from the Gospel narratives, demon-
possession was a very common phenomenon in the ancient
world. Men believed that the air and atmosphere were crowded
with demons, most of them malignant spirits waiting to work
men harm. They believed that the air was so full of them that it
was impossible to insert the point of a needle into the air without
touching one. Some said that there were seven and a half million
of them; some said that there were ten thousand on a man's right
hand and ten thousand on his left. 'The whole world and the cir-
cumambient atmosphere,' as Harnack put it, 'were filled with
devils.'

Various explanations were given of the existence of these
demons. Some said that they had been there in the world since
the beginning of time, always waiting to work men harm. Some
said that they were the spirits of malignant people who had died,
and whose spirits were still going on with their evil and malevolent work. The most common explanation was that they were
the offspring and the descendants of the wicked angels, who
in the old story descended from heaven and seduced mortal
women (Gen. 6.1-8).

It was believed that they could eat and drink, and that they
could beget children, and so propagate their own evil line. They
lived in unclean places, such as tombs. They inhabited places
like deserts where there was no cleansing water. In the lonely

places their howling could be heard, and we still speak of *a howling desert*. They were specially dangerous in the midday heat, and between sunset and sunrise. They specially attacked women in childbirth, the newly-married bride and bridegroom, children who were out after dark, and travellers by night. After dark no one would greet anyone else on the road, lest the greeting be given to a demon. The male demons were known as *shedim* and the female ones, who had long hair, as *lilin* after Lilith. The female demons were specially dangerous to children, and that is why children have their guardian angels (Matt. 18.10).

These demons sought an entry into a man's body. Their commonest way of gaining an entry into a man was to hover round him while he ate and to settle on his food, and so to get inside him. All illness was ascribed to these demons. They entered into a man and seduced him into falling to temptation. They were responsible for mental illness, for madness and for insanity. They were equally responsible for physical illness. The Egyptians believed that there were thirty-six different parts of the human body, and that any of them could be invaded and inhabited by a demon. There were demons of blindness, of deafness, of leprosy, of heart disease, and of every kind of illness and trouble.

The strength of this belief may be seen in a practice cited by A. Rendle Short in his book *The Bible and Modern Medicine*. In many ancient burying-places skulls have been found which have been trepanned, that is to say, skulls which have a small hole bored through them. Clearly in a time when there were no anaesthetics and no real surgical instruments the making of such a hole must have been a very formidable operation. The hole is too small to be of any practical use. The proof that the hole was bored in the lifetime of the person involved is that there is often fresh bone formation round the edges of the hole. The purpose of the trepanning was to release the demon within the man through the hole. The fact that ancient man would submit to such an operation and that ancient doctors would carry it out is proof of how real and intense the belief in demons was in the ancient world. The Ebers Papyrus, discovered in Egypt in 1862, and dating back to 1550 BC, is one of the most ancient medical documents in the world. It has one hundred and eight sections of treatments and prescriptions for all diseases, amongst which there is a prayer to Isis that the patient may be delivered from 'demoniacal and deadly disease'. The treatment of demon-possession was even part of the medical textbooks in the ancient world.

This universal belief in demons had two results. First, if a man was convinced that he was possessed by a demon, that there was a demon settled in any part of his body, then inevitably the physical symptoms of illness would follow, for the belief of the mind always affects the health of the body. The belief and the conviction that he was occupied and possessed by a demon would quite easily make a man's mind mad or paralyse his body. In the ancient world a very great deal of illness was not physical and functional but mental and psychological, and was produced by the belief in the sufferer's mind that he was in the power of some demon. Second, if the belief that he was occupied and possessed by a demon was exorcised from the mind of such a person, then the physical symptoms would depart with the departure of the belief. So long as the man believed that he was possessed by a demon, nothing would cure him, and no treatment would be of any use. But, if his mind was liberated from the belief that he was in the power of a demon, his body and his mind would also at once be liberated from all their pains and their distress. Hence exorcism was a common practice in the ancient world. The belief in demon-possession produced illness, but it also made illness dramatically curable, if the patient could be liberated from the belief.

Two questions will immediately arise. First, is there any such thing as demon-possession? Is demon-possession a reality, or is it a complete delusion? There are those who are not so willing to dismiss demon-possession as nothing but an ancient superstition as once most people were. There are, for instance, types of epilepsy in which there is no morbid pathology of any kind; that is to say, there is no discernible physical reason either in the body or in the brain for the illness; and there are those who wonder if it may not be that there is such a thing as demon-possession after all. But the fact is that, in thinking about the miracles of Jesus, the reality or otherwise of demon-possession is really irrelevant. The one quite certain fact is that the sufferer himself was completely convinced that he was so possessed.

Delusion it might be, nevertheless his belief in it was so complete and absolute that it produced all the symptoms and consequences of physical or mental illness. Demon-possession was an unquestionable reality for the man who believed himself to be suffering from it.

Second, did Jesus believe in demon-possession? To that question there are two answers. It is not in the least likely that the medical and scientific knowledge of Jesus was in any way in advance of his age; all the likelihood is that Jesus did so believe. Further, even if Jesus did not believe in demon-possession, even if he knew that it was a superstitious delusion, it was absolutely necessary for him to assume the patient's belief before he could effect a cure. It would have been pointless for Jesus to tell the sufferer that all his suffering was pure imagination, that the whole condition was a complete delusion, that the madness and the pain and the paralysis were quite unreal. For the patient they *were* real; and Jesus had to assume their reality in order to cure them, even if he himself did not believe in it.

The consequence of all this is that there is not the slightest difficulty for any modern man in believing in any of the miracles which involve the exorcism of demons. The missionary in primitive civilisations is still exorcising demons today. In almost every home we have seen an analogy to this. Illness comes; there is anxiety and alarm; the patient is afraid; those who have no medical knowledge are filled with fear and foreboding as they watch him and try to alleviate his distress. The doctor is sent for. If, as so often happens, the doctor is trusted and respected and even loved not only as physician but as family friend, then the moment the doctor enters the room a new calm comes with him. The fear subsides; the taut nerves relax; confidence returns; the man who can handle things has come. If that can happen with a man, how much more would it happen in the calm, strong presence of Jesus? Jesus' power over the mind of the demon-possessed is something which it is easy to understand. We may well believe that belief in demon-possession is no more than a delusion; we must believe that the symptoms it produced were absolutely real; we have no difficulty in believing that Jesus could restore a demon-possessed man or woman to health of mind and health of body.

Still another factor in the ancient situation was the belief that sin and suffering were indissolubly linked together. It was the firm belief of the Jews that there could be no suffering without some sin to account for it, and that there could be no sin without some suffering to follow from it. When Job was ill and tortured and agonized, his friend Eliphaz said bluntly and accusingly to him: 'Think now, who that was innocent ever perished?' (Job 4.7). This was a basic rabbinic principle, and in his commentary on the Synoptic Gospels C. G. Montefiore cites sayings of the rabbis which illustrate this. Rabbi Ammi said: 'There is no death without guilt, no suffering without sin.' Rabbi Alexandrai said: 'No man gets up from his sickness till God has forgiven all his sins.' Rabbi Hija ben Abba said: 'No sick person is cured from his sickness until all his sins are forgiven.'

There is a sense in which we might well agree with this. The suffering of the world is due to the sin of the world. But we would not make the linkage in the individual human life. We would not say that in every case the individual's suffering is due to the individual's sin. The children often suffer tragically for the sins of the fathers. No man is an isolated unit; we are all bound up together in the bundle of life; every man is involved in the human situation; and again and again his suffering is not due to his own sin but to the sin in which all mankind are involved.

But the Jews rigidly believed this. It is easy to see what could happen, especially in the case of a sensitive person with a tendency towards a kind of morbid self-examination. Such a man might sin; the memory of his sin, the consciousness of his sin, remorse for his sin might take complete possession of him, until it became nothing short of an obsession. He would well know the orthodox connection between sin and suffering. And it would almost inevitably happen that he would think himself, will himself, believe himself into serious illness in which distress would lodge in his mind and pain or paralysis within his body.

To cure such a man, the first thing essential would be to assure him of the forgiveness of his sins. Until he had that assurance, nothing would remove his physical or mental illness; once he had that assurance his mental or physical symptoms would vanish like the night before the dawn. That is precisely why Jesus began one of his most notable miracles by saying to the sufferer: 'My son, your sins are forgiven' (Mark 2.1-12; Matt. 9.1-8; Luke 5.18-26). The assurance of forgiveness was the one thing necessary to shatter the self-imposed bonds of pain which the conscience of the sufferer had imposed upon himself.

In this approach to the sufferer Jesus was entirely at one with modern medicine. Paul Tournier in *A Doctor's Case Book* quotes an illustration of this kind of thing from his own experience. One of his friends had as a patient a girl suffering from anaemia. No treatment had any success. He sent her to the medical officer of the district with a view to having her accepted as a patient in a mountain sanatorium. The medical officer granted the application, but he wrote to the doctor: 'On analysing the blood, however, I do not arrive at anything like the figures you quote.' The doctor did not doubt his own analysis; but he took a fresh sample of the blood, tested it in his own laboratory, and found to his astonishment that the blood count had completely changed. He knew that he had made no mistake in either this or his former tests. Why the change? He sent for the girl. 'Has anything out of the ordinary happened in your life,' he asked, 'since your last visit?' 'Yes, something has happened,' she replied. 'I have suddenly been able to forgive some one against whom I bore a nasty grudge; and all at once I felt as if I could at last say "Yes" to life!' Her mental attitude had changed her whole bodily condition. The removal of the resentment and the consequent removal of the subconscious feeling of guilt had changed the whole matter. The girl was now at peace with God and at peace with her fellow-human-beings—and health came back.

In any situation in which the idea of sin and the idea of suffering have become intertwined and dependent on each other, it is the sense of guilt which brings the illness, whether the illness be physical or mental; and, if the sense of guilt is removed, if the assurance of forgiveness is received, then the illness will disappear. It is easy to understand how Jesus was able to restore people to health and strength of body and of mind by assuring them of the forgiveness of sins.

It is of interest to note that a well-known psychiatrist has said that he seldom has Roman Catholics amongst his patients. Even if we admit that a Roman Catholic would sooner go to a priest than to a psychiatrist, the fact remains suggestive. The psychiatrist attributed this to the fact that the Roman Catholic is in the habit of confessing his sins and of then receiving absolution for them; and he suggested that the Protestant churches should not only condemn sin, should not only urge the confession of sin in prayer, but should also in no uncertain voice proclaim the fact that in Jesus Christ we *are* forgiven. If the prayer of confession ended with the proclamation of forgiveness, it might well relax the tension in many a mind and body distressed by the consciousness of sin.

When we are thinking of the stories of the miracles of Jesus, we must take into account still another characteristic of the Hebrew mind. The Hebrew seldom or never thought of things, or explained events, in terms of what we would call secondary causes. We would say that certain atmospheric conditions caused the thunder, the lightning or the rain; the Hebrew would simply say that God sent the thunder, the lightning or the rain. We would say that certain weather conditions caused the failure of crops. The Hebrew would say that God sent blasting and mildew and caused a famine. We would say that certain unhygienic practices and certain insanitary conditions caused an epidemic of illness in a place. The Hebrew would say that God had sent a plague upon the people. We habitually ascribe events and conditions to secondary causes; the Hebrew just as habitually ascribed them to God.

It so happens that there is a piece of Hebrew history which is described from three different points of view by three different historians from three different countries. Few events in ancient history made such an impression on men's minds as the disastrous withdrawal of Sennacherib from his attack on Palestine and on Jerusalem. The Old Testament historian describes that event: 'And that night the angel of the Lord went forth, and slew an hundred and eighty-five thousand in the camp of the Assyrians, and when men arose early in the morning, behold these were all dead bodies. Then Sennacherib king of Assyria departed, and went home, and dwelt at Nineveh' (II Kings 19.35f.).

The Greek historian Herodotus[1] hands down the Egyptian

---

[1]   Herodotus 2.141.

version of the same story. The people were in terror. Sethos the priest prayed for deliverance. The god told the people not to fear and said: 'Myself will send you a champion.' So, the story goes on, one night a multitude of fieldmice swarmed over the Assyrian encampment, and devoured their quivers and their bowstrings and the handles of their spears, and the enemy fled unarmed, and many perished. So, Herodotus goes on to say, to this day in the Temple of Hephaestus in Egypt there is a statue of the Egyptian king with a mouse in his hand with the words: 'Look on me and fear the gods.'

The third account of the same incident is in the work of Berosus, a Chaldaean historian, and it is handed down to us by Josephus.[1] He says quite simply that 'a pestilential distemper' came upon the army of the Assyrian king. The king was in great dread and terrible agony at this calamity, and in his fear he fled back to his own kingdom with his surviving forces.

Here, then, are the three accounts. The Hebrew account says that the angel of the Lord caused the destruction; the Egyptian account says that mice caused it; the Chaldaean account says that a terrible pestilence caused it. Which is right? All three are right. Rats and mice are notorious carriers of plague, especially of bubonic plague. What happened was that a terrible outbreak of plague fell upon the Assyrian armies, and they were forced all unexpectedly back to their own country. The Egyptian and the Chaldaean historians had some idea of secondary causes; the Hebrew historian described the event as the direct action of God.

It is quite clear that anyone who thought as the Hebrews thought would see God's hand in all kinds of events for which others would find a natural explanation. The Hebrew would not, for instance, ascribe the cure of a disease or an illness to a physician or a surgeon, but direct to God. And who shall say that the Hebrew was wrong, for did not a great doctor say, 'I only bandage men's wounds—God heals them'? It is clear that there is far more room for the conception of the miraculous in a world such as the Hebrew believed in than in the kind of world in which we believe. A miracle has been described as 'the will

[1] *Antiquities* 10.1.5.

of God expressed in natural events'. It may be that the Hebrew was more right than we think, and that there are more miracles in this world than our earthbound philosophy recognizes.

In seeking to understand the miracles of Jesus there is one other factor which we must take into account. It must be obvious that we cannot see anything as some one else sees it, unless we see it from his standpoint and from his viewpoint. With the single exception of Luke all the New Testament writers were Jews; they, therefore, saw events through Jewish eyes. If, then, we try to interpret their writings in terms of modern Western thought we are bound to distort it. We must, as far as we can, think ourselves back to their position. When we do that, we come upon one consistent principle of Jewish writing and teaching. No Jewish teacher would ask of any story: 'Did this literally happen?' He would ask: 'What does this teach?' C. J. Ball sums up the rabbinic method of teaching and of interpretation:

> We have to bear in mind a fact familiar enough to students of Talmudic and Midrashic literature . . . the inveterate tendency of Jewish teachers to convey their doctrine, not in the form of abstract discourse, but in a mode appealing directly to the imagination, and seeking to arouse the interest and sympathy of the man rather than the philosopher. The Rabbi embodies his lesson in a story, whether parable or allegory or seeming historical narrative; and the last thing he or his disciples would think of is to ask whether the selected persons, events and circumstances which so vividly suggest the doctrine are in themselves real or fictitious. The doctrine is everything; the mode of presentation has no independent value. To make the story the first consideration, and the doctrine it was intended to convey an afterthought as we, with our dry Western literalness, are predisposed to do, is to reverse the Jewish order of thinking, and to do unconscious injustice to the authors of many edifying narratives of antiquity.[1]

This is to say that Jewish teachers were more concerned with truth than with fact. They are not interested in the momentary

[1] Introduction to the Song of the Three Children, *Speaker's Commentary, Apocrypha*, Vol. II, p. 307.

historical events of any story; they are interested only in the eternal truth which the story is designed to illuminate and to convey.

We are not entirely unfamiliar with this way of thinking. When we read the *Pilgrim's Progress* we do not ask whether these persons literally lived, or whether the events happened at a given time in a given place in the world of space and time; we ask what is the eternal truth that this story is seeking to convey to us about God and man.

We must seek to read the miracle stories of the Gospels with the same eyes as those who wrote them. We must not apply to them the same standards as we would apply to the narrative of a modern Western historian or of a newspaper report. Unless we understand why and how they were written, we shall not understand what they were designed to teach us, and we shall often lose the precious kernel through over-concern for the husk.

The Greek words which are used for the miracles of Jesus are in themselves expressive of the character and the nature of the miracles. Three words are used for the miracles in the New Testament.

The miracles are called *dunameis,* which means 'works of power' (Matt. 11.20-23; 13.54,58; Mark 6.2,5; Luke 10.13; 19.37). It is said of Jesus that the power *(dunamis)* of the Lord was with him to heal (Luke 5.17). It is said that power *(dunamis)* came forth from him, and he healed them all (Luke 6.19). And this was a power of which Jesus was conscious, for, when he was touched in the crowd by the woman with the issue of blood, he was conscious that power had gone out of him (Mark 5.30; Luke 8.46). From this word we learn that the miracles are the irruption of divine power into the human situation for help and healing.

The word *teras* is used to describe the miracles, but it is never used alone. In the Gospels *teras* is not used at all of the miracles of Jesus, although it is used of the astonishing things that the false Christs would do (Matt. 24.24; Mark 13.22). *Teras* means something which produces wonder and amazement and astonishment. The word *teras* has no kind of moral quality. A conjuring trick could be a *teras,* for a *teras* is only something which produces amazement.

As we have said, *teras* is never used alone to describe the miracles of Jesus; when it is used, it is used along with *sēmeion*, which means 'a sign'. In Acts Jesus' miracles are said to be *signs and wonders* (Acts 2.22), and *signs and wonders* were frequent phenomena in the life of the early Church (Acts 2.43; 4.30; 5.12; 6.8; 14.3; 15.12). The word *sēmeion* is the characteristic word for the miracles of Jesus in the Fourth Gospel, although it is not used in the first three Gospels (John 2.11,23; 3.2; 4.54; 6.2; 7.31; 9.16; 11.47; 12.18; 20.30).

It is the word *sēmeion* which really describes the miracles of Jesus. A *sēmeion* is a sign; it is a significant event; it is an action which reveals the mind and character of the person who performs it; it is an outward action designed to allow him who sees it to see into the inner mind and heart of him who performs it. Above all the miracles were events which revealed the mind and the heart of Jesus, and, through him, the mind and heart of God.

Of what, then, are the miracles of Jesus the sign and the revelation? They are the revelation of two things. They are, as we have already seen, the revelation of *power*. In them we see in action a power which is able to deal with the human situation, a power through which pain and suffering can be defeated, a power through which sin, and the consequences of sin, can be overcome. They are the revelation of *pity*. Again and again it is said of Jesus that he was *moved with compassion*, either for the crowds or for some sufferer (Matt. 9.36; 14.14; 15.32; 20.34; Mark 1.41; 6.34; 8.2; Luke 7.13). The word is *splagchnizesthai*, which is the strongest word in Greek for the experience of pity and compassion. *Splagchna* are the bowels, and the word describes the pity and compassion which move a man to the depths of his being. The miracles, therefore, are the sign of power and pity in the heart of Jesus, and therefore in the heart of God. They are the sign that God cares, and that God can make his care effective. They are the sign that the power of God is used in pity, and that the pity of God is backed by power. In the miracles we see the power and the pity of God combine to deal with the human situation.

Having sketched the background against which the miracles of Jesus happened, and having accepted the basic fact that they are signs of the power and the pity of God, exercised in love for men, we can now go on to look at the miracles themselves. When we do so, we find that the miracles of Jesus fall into four different classes. There may sometimes be doubt and debate into which of these classes any individual miracle falls, but the four classes do cover the miracles.

(i) *There are acts and healings which are beyond our comprehension.* It is inevitable that that should be so. The unique quality of Jesus is his sinlessness. It may well be that *sinlessness* is an inadequate term in which to describe Jesus, for the word itself is a negative word rather than a positive one, and might well be interpreted in terms of refraining from doing things rather than in terms of positive action. But this remains true—if Jesus was sinless, it means that in every decision and action of life he knew, accepted and acted on the will of God; he rendered to God a continuous and a unique obedience. If that is so, it is quite clear that Jesus could both develop and be entrusted with powers such as ordinary persons cannot possess. If an ordinary person were entrusted with the power of working miracles, it is certain that he would do more harm than good. He would be bound to use such power in ignorance, and therefore unwisely. He would be bound to use it in essential human selfishness, and therefore dangerously. The great problem of the present human situation, in which men control powers which can disintegrate the very universe, is in fact that men possess power which they are neither spiritually nor morally fitted to control. Their achievement in the world of science has outstripped their growth in the world of the spirit.

The Greeks told their story of a good and simple man called Gyges, who lived a kind and an upright and honest life. By chance he entered into possession of the ring which gave him the power of being invisible, and he straightway embarked on something very like a career of crime. He had acquired a power which he was not fit to use.

The fact that for Jesus there was no other rule of life than the will of God made it possible for him to receive and to acquire powers which would have been safe in the hands of no other person.

(ii) *There are miracle stories which must be interpreted in*

*the light of the vivid Eastern way of putting things, and which
are in fact stories of quite natural happenings told as an Oriental
would tell them.*

The best example of that type of story is the story of the coin
in the fish's mouth (Matt. 17.24-27). The time had come to pay
the Temple tax, which every Jew must pay. The tax was half a
shekel, which was equal to two drachmae, a sum equal to about
one shilling and sixpence. This sum must be evaluated against
the fact that a working man's wage in Palestine was about eight-
pence per day. For a Palestinian peasant half a shekel was a
considerable sum. So, as the story runs, Jesus said to Peter: 'Go
and catch a fish. In the fish's mouth you will find a piece of
money enough to pay our joint tax. Take it, and go and pay the
Temple tax for yourself and for me.'

If we insist on taking that story literally, we are confronted
with a series of difficulties. First, the whole event is a *teras;* it is
simply an amazing and astonishing happening with no moral
significance whatever. Second, it represents Jesus as doing what
he never did, what he in fact absolutely refused to do, what in
fact he rejected once and for all at the time of his temptations;
it represents him as using his power for his own benefit and for
his own convenience. If this story is to be taken literally, it is the
one and only occasion on which Jesus used his power to profit
himself. Third, if the story is taken literally, it tells of a very
easy way out of a practical difficulty. Life would be very much
easier, if we could pay our just and legitimate debts by finding
coins in fishes' mouths. It would in fact be a quite immoral and
unethical way in which to gain money, and would be an incentive
to laziness and to shiftlessness. Fourth, if the story is to be taken
literally, it has no point at all for us today. It sets us no example
and brings us no challenge and establishes no Christian principle.
It is simply a wonder story.

What, then did happen? This we regard as an essential question, for we strongly believe that no miracle story is a baseless
invention and fiction, but that every miracle story goes back to
some actual event. We must remember the Eastern delight in
vivid narration; and we must also remember that Jesus often
taught with a smile and with a flash of humour, which clothed
the truth in the sunshine of laughter. Surely what Jesus said was

something like this: 'Peter, the Temple tax is due. We haven't any money, and we must pay it, for we must fulfil all our lawful obligations. Well, then, away back to the boats for a day! Get out the nets, the lines, the bait! We need the money, and you'll get it in the fishes' mouths!' This is Jesus saying with a wit that made the saying memorable: 'Meet your obligations from your day's work.'

Here there is something which is immediately relevant. If the story is taken literally as telling of the finding of a coin in a fish's mouth, whereby a just debt was paid, then the story has nothing to do with us, for we will never pay our debts that way, nor would it be good for us if we could; but if the story says to us, 'Pay your debts by doing an honest day's work,' then the story speaks to our situation.

It will mean that the shop assistant finds the necessary money for life in the work of the counter on which she serves; that the garage mechanic will find it in the cylinders and the pistons of the car that he is repairing or servicing; that the typist and the author will find pound notes in the keys of the typewriter; that the plumber will find silver in his blowlamp and in his solder; that the wireless engineer will find it amongst his valves and transformers and condensers. This story will say to us that Christian diligence and Christian efficiency are the way to pay our debts and to meet the needs of life. Taken with a crude and humourless and uncomprehending literalness, this is only a wonder story with nothing to say to us for life; taken with imagination and insight and an appreciation of the way in which the mind of an Eastern teacher works, this is a story which gives us a recipe for life and living.

(iii) *There are a large number of Jesus' miracles which, at least in principle, it is not difficult to understand; for it is difficult to see why anyone should have any great difficulty in accepting the healing miracles of Jesus.*

In a world in which illness was connected with demon-possession and with the consequences and the results of sin, it is easy to see how the impact of a calm strong personality could break the belief in demons, and how a word of grace and of authority could convince of forgiveness, and how health of body and of mind could thus be restored. We ourselves know well the peace and the calm which can come to us in trouble on the arrival of some one whom we respect and trust and love, and whom we know to be able to cope with the situation. We know, and are continually coming to know better, how closely body, mind and spirit are interconnected; we have experienced the power of the impact of an authoritative and beloved personality upon us; and we have no difficulty in understanding how the presence and the power of the personality of Jesus released men from the pains and distresses of body and of mind which their own fears and superstitions had brought upon them. There are few things in the Gospel narrative easier to believe and to accept than the fact that Jesus healed the bodies and the minds of men.

(iv) *There are certain miracle stories—and they are the most precious and important of all—which are not so much designed to tell us the story of a single incident as to enshrine and to embody an eternal truth.* They are indeed *sēmeia,* signs which enable us to see, not so much what Jesus did, as what Jesus does. And, if it be insisted that such stories be taken with crude and stubborn literalism, then the greater part of their value and meaning is lost. To illustrate this, we shall take the greatest of these stories, the story of the raising of Lazarus (John 11.1-44).

If this story is taken as a literal account of a raising from the dead, we have to ask the question, Why did the other Gospel writers omit it, especially when John implies that it was the moving cause of the Crucifixion (John 11.47-54)? There can be no doubt that this story goes back to some notable event in the life and the ministry of Jesus—but to what?

The story clearly centres round one saying, for the sake of which the story exists: 'I am the resurrection and the life; he who believes in me, though he die, yet shall he live; and he that liveth and believeth in me shall never die' (John 11.25f.). The story is the casket which contains that gem; the story is the presentation of Jesus as the Resurrection and the Life. But nothing can be clearer than that the saying is not *physically and literally true.* 'He who believes in me, though he die, yet shall he live'—but he who believes in Jesus Christ does *not* come back to physical life within this world of space and time. 'Whoever lives and believes in me shall never die'—but death is *not* arrested for the man who believes in Jesus Christ; the hurrying years do not wait for him. Death in the physical and literal sense of the term comes to him as surely as it comes to every man. As Epicurus long ago had it, in regard to death we mortals all live in an unfortified city. Taken physically and literally, that great saying of Jesus is not true. If it be taken physically and literally Jesus is in fact promising something which he cannot and does not perform. But taken spiritually, this saying is blessedly and profoundly and gloriously true. Spiritually the Christian is abundantly armed against all death's endeavours. Spiritually the Christian is gloriously saved from the death of sin and raised to newness of life.

If this saying of Jesus must be taken in a spiritual sense, then it is clear that we must take the whole story in a spiritual sense. Surely what is meant is something like this. Lazarus had committed some terrible sin, a sin which had brought to the home at Bethany a grief like the grief for death, a sin which he would never have committed, if Jesus had been present, a sin which had made his name stink in the nostrils of men, a sin which had broken the hearts of his sisters, a sin which had left him spiritually dead, and even unable to repent. Then comes Jesus—and all is healed and all is changed. Lazarus is raised to life anew. Once again Jesus had shown himself the friend of sinners, to the amazed joy of Martha and Mary and Lazarus, and to the bitter resentment and cold criticism and venomous hatred of the orthodox good people of his day. Surely this is the supreme conversion story of the New Testament.

If we want some parallel to this, we get it in the words of Paul. 'For I through the law am dead to the law, that I might live unto God. I am crucified with Christ' (Gal. 2.19-21). We know that Paul was not *physically* dead; we know very well that he was not *literally* crucified; and we also know that it is gloriously true that out of the frustration and death of sin, he rose through Jesus Christ to the wonder and the glory of new life.

If this story is simply the story of the raising of a dead man in the village of Bethany somewhere about the year AD 28 or 29, then it has nothing to do with us; it cannot and it does not happen now; but if it is the story of the defeat of the death caused by sin, then it is telling of something which Jesus Christ can do, and does, every day in life.

In *The Bible Speaks to You,* Robert McAfee Brown tells how he was chaplain on a troopship on which 1,500 American Marines were returning to America from Japan for discharge. To his surprise and delight a group of them came to him with a request for Bible Study. Towards the end of the trip they were studying John 11. Professor Brown was thinking within himself: 'What are these men making of this, "I am the Resurrection and the Life"? The question is not, "Was a corpse reanimated in AD 30?" but, "Are these words true in AD 1946?" ' At the end of the study a young marine came to him. He said something like this: 'Padre, everything in this story we have been studying today points to me. I've been in hell for the last six months, and since I have heard this chapter I am just getting free.' He went on to explain. He had gone into the Marines straight from college, and had been sent overseas to Japan. He had been bored and had gone out to find amusement and had got into trouble, bad trouble. No one knew about it—*but God knew about it.* He had a terrible feeling of guilt. He felt that his life was ruined. He felt he could never again face his family, even if they never knew the wretched story. 'I've been a dead man,' he said, 'condemned by myself, condemned by my family, if they knew. But, after reading this chapter, I'm alive again.' He went on: 'The Resurrection and the Life that Jesus was talking about is the real thing here and now.' That lad had a hard job to get things put straight again, but he did it, for, when life seemed ended for him, and when he seemed a dead man, Jesus raised him to life anew, out of a life which sin had killed. And that is exactly what this story means.

Let no man think that such an approach to the miracles of Jesus is either negative or destructive. The aim is not to explain away the miracles; the aim is to appropriate the miracles. There is little use in a Jesus who *did* things almost two thousand years ago, but who has ceased to do them now. What we need is a Christ who still *does* things. There is little relevance in the story of a Jesus who raised a dead man to life in Bethany nineteen hundred years ago, but who never does that now; there is every relevance in a Christ who to this day daily raises men from the death of sin and liberates them to life eternal. There is little relevance in a Jesus who stilled a storm on the Sea of Galilee nineteen hundred years ago, and who stills no storms today, for there are those whose loved ones have been taken by the storms in spite of the most intense prayers; there is every relevance in a Christ who stills the storms which rise within the hearts of men today, and in whose presence today every storm becomes a calm within the heart. There is a little relevance in a Jesus who turned water into wine nineteen hundred years ago, and who never does so today; there is every relevance in a Jesus in whose presence today there enters into life a new quality of radiance and joy and exhilaration which is like the turning of water into wine.

We believe that when these stories are read in a spirit of crude and unimaginative literalism, they lose almost all their value; we believe that many of them are not meant to describe literal happenings, but are meant to describe spiritual changes and experiences which are still triumphantly happening in the power of the risen Lord. They are presenting eternal truth in a picture, and they tell, not of things which *happened,* but of things which *happen.*

In the miracle stories we see demonstrated the power and the pity of God exercised in love for men, and by many of them we are intended to see, not, for instance, a storm stilled on the Sea of Galilee, but a storm stilled in the hearts of men even in the midst of a terrifying upheaval, the record not of an act of Jesus, but the sign of the continuing action of Christ, not the record of an event to be read about, but the record of an experience offered still to be enjoyed.

10

THE MASTER TEACHER

EVEN if Jesus had no other claim to be remembered, he would be remembered as one of the world's masters of the technique of teaching. 'Teacher' was a title which even his enemies were prepared to concede to him. When they came to him with a testing question, they began by saying: 'Teacher, we know that you are true, and teach the way of God truthfully' (Matt. 22.16; Mark 12.14; Luke 20.21).

The frequency with which Jesus was called *teacher* is concealed by the fact that the Authorized Version consistently translated the Greek word for teacher by the English word 'master', using 'master' in the sense in which we speak of a 'schoolmaster'. There are three titles applied to Jesus in the Gospels all of which describe him as a teacher. The commonest is *didaskalos,* which is used of him almost forty times. This is the word which the Authorized Version translates 'master'; to read the Gospels in the Revised Standard Version or in the Moffatt translation is to see how often the word 'teacher' is applied to Jesus. Luke uses the word *epistatēs* (Luke 5.5; 8.24,45; 9.33,49; 17.13). This is the word which would be used in secular Greek for a headmaster. Sometimes the Gospel writers retain the word *Rabbi* (Matt. 26.49; Mark 9.5; 10.51; 11.21; 14.45). *Rabbi* literally means 'My great one', and was the standard Jewish title for a distinguished and acknowledged teacher. It would be the word by which Jesus was most commonly addressed, and *didaskalos* and *epistatēs* are both translations into Greek of the title *Rabbi*. When we put the three titles together, and when we remember that they all represent and go back to the word *Rabbi,* the standard word for an accepted teacher, we find that in the narrow space of the Gospel narratives Jesus is called 'teacher' more than fifty times. The New Testament presents us with the picture of Jesus as the teacher *par excellence*.

In the conditions in which he taught Jesus had certain problems to face, and the way in which he met the challenge of these problems is a demonstration of his greatness as a teacher.

(i) It is true that Jesus began his teaching in the synagogues of Galilee, but before long the opposition and the hatred of the orthodox religious authorities of his day had shut the door of the synagogue against him, and driven him out to the roads, and the hillside, and the seashore. By far the greater part of his teaching was done in the open air. It was field preaching. In the great early days of Methodism John Wesley could write: 'Our societies were formed from those who were wandering upon the dark mountains, that belonged to no Christian Church; but were awakened by the preaching of the Methodists, who had pursued them through the wilderness of this world to the Highways and the Hedges—to the Markets and the Fairs—to the Hills and the Dales—who set up the Standard of the Cross in the Streets and Lanes of the Cities, in the Villages, in the Barns, and Farmers' Kitchens etc.—and all this in such a way, and to such an extent, as never had been done before, since the Apostolic age.' That was a repetition of the preaching of Jesus.

All teaching which is done in the open air demands one outstanding quality—it must be *immediately arresting*. He who preaches in a pulpit, or lectures in a college, or teaches in a schoolroom, has one initial advantage. He has an audience who cannot get up and move away when they wish! But the teacher in the open air has first to persuade men to stop and then to persuade them to stay. His teaching must be immediately arresting, or he will never collect an audience, or, having collected an audience, he will never retain it.

(ii) He who would teach in the open air must have *a universal appeal*. In a church or a class room or a lecture hall the preacher or teacher will have a more or less homogeneous audience; but in the open air the hearers will be of every kind. One of the most amazing characteristics of Jesus as a teacher is the universality of his appeal. We find him teaching in the synagogues (Matt. 4.23; Luke 4.15). We find him teaching in the Temple at Jerusalem (Mark 14.49; Matt. 26.55; Luke 20.1). We find him engaged in technical arguments and discussion with the foremost scholars of his day (Matt. 22.23-46; Mark 12.13-44; Luke 20.19-44). We find him in the streets and on the roads, using a fishing-boat as a pulpit by the seashore, holding the crowds spellbound with his words (Matt. 11.1; Mark 2.13; 4.1;

Luke 5.17). We find him teaching the intimate inner circle of the disciples (Matt. 5.1; Mark 8.31), and yet we find that amidst the crowds the common people heard him gladly (Mark 12.37).

This is extraordinary teaching. There is many a teacher who is very effective in the pulpit of a church but quite ineffective with a crowd at the gates of a shipyard or a factory. There is many a man quite at home on the rostrum of a class room but quite unable to make his message intelligible to the ordinary man and woman. There are men whom the crowds will gladly hear but who would be lost in the more rarified atmosphere of the academic world. There have been very few teachers who were equally at home and equally effective with any kind of audience—but Jesus was. As a teacher he had in a unique degree the quality of universal appeal.

(iii) He who would teach and preach to crowds in the open air must have the gift of being *immediately intelligible*. If a man is learning by reading a book, when he comes on a difficult sentence or on an idea or a passage that he does not immediately understand, he can halt and go back over it and linger on it until he has elucidated it and grasped its meaning. But he who is learning by listening cannot do that. If the hearer does not grasp immediately the meaning of what is being said, he loses the thread of the argument; or he begins to puzzle about the difficult sentence and its meaning, and so loses what follows, and cannot catch up again. The man who would teach crowds in the open air must have a limpid lucidity and a transparent simplicity which make it almost impossible to mistake what he is saying. One of the great characteristics of the teaching of Jesus is that, however much men might disagree with it, he never left anyone in any doubt what he was saying and demanding.

(iv) To be arresting, to be universal in appeal, to be immediately intelligible—these are demands made upon any open air preacher to mixed crowds. But Jesus was faced with still another problem. His message had to be *permanently memorable*. Jesus taught in times long before there was any such thing as a printed book, and when handwritten manuscripts were rare and expensive. In modern conditions a teacher may hope that, even if what he is saying is forgotten, it may always be recovered and rediscovered in the printed word. He can always hand to those whom he teaches a permanent record in print of that which he teaches. He can refer, and point his readers, to books which contain and explain what he has been saying. It was not possible for Jesus to do that. He had to teach in such a way that he immediately printed his message permanently and indelibly on the minds of his hearers. That is to say, he had not only to find a message, but he had to find an unforgettable form in which to express his message.

So, then, Jesus had to solve the problem of teaching in such a way that his message was immediately arresting, universally appealing, immediately intelligible and permanently memorable. Let us now see how he solved the problem.

(i) Jesus used *the unforgettable epigram*, the phrase which lodges in the mind and stays there, refusing to be forgotten, even when the mind would willingly forget it.

> Whoever exalts himself will be humbled, and whoever humbles himself will be exalted (Matt. 23.12; Luke 18.14).

> A man's life does not consist in the abundance of his possessions (Luke 12.15).

> No one who puts his hand to the plough and looks back is fit for the kingdom of God (Luke 9.62).

> Whoever would save his life will lose it, and whoever loses his life for my sake will find it (Matt. 16.25).

> What will it profit a man, if he gains the whole world and forfeits his life? Or what shall a man give in return for his life? (Matt. 16.26).

Such sayings have the gadfly of truth in them. Their supreme quality is that they will not leave a man alone. He cannot forget them. Every now and then they flash unbidden into his mind. Even when he would willingly forget them, they flash across the screen of his memory and leave him thinking and wondering. Often Jesus taught in sayings which refuse to be forgotten.

(ii) Jesus used *the thought-provoking paradox*. He said things which on the face of it sounded incredible, but which somehow haunt the mind and the heart with the lurking suspicion that after all they may be true. This is specially true of the Beatitudes (Matt. 5.1-16; Luke 6.20-26). Blessed are the poor, the hungry, the sorrowful, the persecuted. Every one of them bluntly and flatly contradicts the world's standards and the world's measurements; here is a reversal of all that is accepted as worldly and prudential wisdom, a turning of life upside down. Unless a man becomes like a little child, he cannot enter the Kingdom of Heaven (Matt. 18.3). Herein all the worldly standards of greatness and of prestige are annihilated in a sentence.

The great value of these sayings is their long-term disturbing power. When a man first hears them, he may well dismiss them as fantastic and unreal and incredible and untrue. But something has been dropped into his mind which even against his will compels him to think, and, if he goes on thinking for long enough, conclusions will force themselves upon him, even if he does not wish them to be true. In many ways Jesus is the great disturber, and not least in these thought-compelling paradoxes which he dropped into the minds and hearts of men.

(iii)   Jesus used the *vivid hyperbole*. There are times when men need shock treatment, if they are to see the truth. They must be taken and shaken out of their comfortable lethargy. 'If your right eye,' said Jesus, 'causes you to sin, pluck it out and throw it away. If your right hand is opening the way to temptation, cut it off and hurl it from you' (Matt. 5.29f.; Mark 9.43-48). 'If any man comes to me, and does not hate his own father and mother and wife and children and brothers and sisters, yes, and even his own life, he cannot be my disciple' (Luke 14.26). Literalism is here forbidden, for this is the language of poetry and of passion. Sometimes a picture has to be overdrawn, if men are to see it at all. Jesus never hesitated to say the most shattering things in order to stab men broad awake, so that even against their will the light of the truth would banish the unseeing slumber from their eyes.

(iv)   Jesus used *penetrating humour*. Horace, the Roman poet, in a famous phrase, spoke of speaking the truth with a smile.[1] Often truth spoken with a smile will penetrate the mind and reach the heart; the lesson strikes home without wounding because of the wit in the saying. It was this form of teaching

[1]   *Ridentem dicere verum:* Horace, *Satires* 1.1.24.

that Jesus used when he was speaking of the folly of criticizing and finding fault with each other, and when he drew a picture of a man with a plank in his own eye seeking to extract a speck of dust from the eye of some one else (Matt. 7.1-5).

'Laughter,' said Thomas Hobbes, 'is nothing else but sudden glory.' 'Let your speech,' said Paul, 'always be gracious, seasoned with salt' (Col. 4.6). And C. F. D. Moule comments that this verse may well be 'a plea to Christians not to confuse loyal godliness with a dull, graceless insipidity'. It has been all too true that too often in Christian teaching laughter has been a heresy and seriousness has been identified with gloom. Jesus knew that often the way to the heart of an audience is through a smile; and he said things which at the moment made men laugh, but which, when they thought about them, left them face to face with the gravity of truth.

(v) The teaching instrument which is above all connected with the name of Jesus is the parable. To teach by parables is to teach by story-telling, for a parable may be well described as 'an earthly story with a heavenly meaning'. If Jesus had no other claim to fame, he would rank as one of the supreme constructors of the short story. As a teaching instrument the parable has three great advantages.

(a) The parable, the story, is the teaching instrument which all men know, and which the Jews especially used. From childhood men say: 'Tell me a story.' Sir Philip Sidney spoke of 'a tale which holdeth children from play and old men from the chimney corner'. In the Old Testament there is Nathan's courageous parable to warn David of his sin (II Sam. 12.1-7), and Isaiah's parable with the picture of the nation of Israel as the vineyard of the Lord (Isa. 5.1-7).

The Jewish rabbis knew and used the parable in their teaching. There is, for instance, a very beautiful rabbinic parable which tells why God chose Moses as the leader of his people. 'When Moses was feeding the sheep of his father-in-law in the wilderness, a young kid ran away. Moses followed it until it reached a ravine, where it found a well from which to drink. When Moses came up to it he said: "I did not know that you ran away because you were thirsty. Now you must be weary." So he took the kid on his shoulders and carried it back. Then God said: "Because you have shown pity to one of a flock belonging to a man, you shall lead my flock Israel." '

When Jesus used the parable, he was using the method of teaching which all men know from their childhood, and which the Jewish teachers had always known and loved.

(b) To teach in parables is to teach in pictures, and most men think in pictures. There are very few people who are capable of grasping abstract truth; for most men truth has to become concrete before it becomes intelligible. We might, for instance, labour long and ineffectively to define the abstract idea of beauty, but, if we can point at a person, and say, 'That is a beautiful person,' then the abstract idea becomes clear.

It is not only *The Word* which must become flesh; every great idea must become flesh, every great word must become a person, before men can grasp and understand it. So, for instance, when Paul speaks about faith, he does not enter into a long and abstract discussion and definition. He draws the living picture of Abraham. In Abraham faith becomes flesh; the abstract becomes concrete; the idea becomes a picture and a person.

That is why the story is the most universal form of teaching— and Jesus was a master of that method without an equal.

(c) The parable has in it the characteristic approach of Jesus to teaching. The parable does not so much *tell* a man the truth as it enables a man to *discover* the truth for himself. The parable says to a man, 'It is like this . . . Think of it this way . . .' and then leaves him to draw his own conclusions and to make his own deductions. Truth which is merely told is quick to be forgotten; truth which is discovered lasts a lifetime. Truth can never be inserted into a man like a pill or an injection; truth is like a goal to which a man's mind under the guidance and the stimulus of God must journey in its own seeking.

The great value of the parable is that it does not impose truth on a man; it puts a man in a position in which he can go on to discover, or to realize, truth for himself. A parable has the double power of opening a man's mind to new truth, and of making him aware of truth which he already knows, but the relevance of which he has failed to see.

In all his teaching Jesus moved from 'the here and now' to 'the there and then'. He began on earth to reach heaven; he began in time to end in eternity; he began from where men are to lead men to where they ought to be. He began from the corn growing in the cornfield, from a woman baking in a cottage kitchen, from a coin lost in the rushes which strewed a living-room floor, from a sheep which had wandered away, from a son who had run away, from an everyday incident of assault and robbery on the Jerusalem to Jericho road. Jesus could do that because for him the world is 'the garment of the living God'. He knew that the visible things of this world were designed to enable us to see through them and beyond them to the invisible things (Rom. 1.20). As William Temple put it: 'Jesus taught men to see the operation of God in the regular and the normal— in the rising of the sun and the falling of the rain and the growth of the plant.' Everything in God's world was to him a road to lead men's thoughts to God.

(vi) We may finally note that in his teaching Jesus used three forms of logical argument, as W. A. Curtis has pointed out.

(a) He used the *reductio ad absurdum*. He was accused of casting out devils by the help of the prince of devils. His answer was: 'How can Satan cast out Satan? If a kingdom is divided against itself, that kingdom cannot stand. And if a house is divided against itself, that house will not be able to stand. And if Satan has risen up against himself and is divided, he cannot stand, but is coming to an end' (Mark 3.23-26). With one shrewd blow Jesus reduced the charge of his opponents to an absurdity.

(b) He used the *logical dilemma*. He did not break out in railing rebuke against those who brought to him the woman taken in adultery. He simply said quietly: 'Let him who is with-out sin among you be the first to throw a stone at her' (John 8.7). When they accused him of breaking the Sabbath day by healing on it, and when he knew that they were seeking to find a way in which to kill him, he faced them with the question: 'Is it law-ful on the sabbath to do good or to do harm, to save a life or to kill?' (Mark 3.4). He silenced his opponents by impaling them on the horns of a dilemma.

(c) He used the *argument a fortiori*. 'If you then,' he said, 'who are evil, know how to give good gifts to your children, *how much more* will your Father who is in heaven give good things to those who ask him?' (Matt. 7.11). 'If,' he said, 'God so clothes the grass of the field, which today is alive and tomorrow is thrown into the oven, will he not *much more* clothe you, O men of little faith?' (Matt. 6.30).

There are many men who genuinely have something to say, and who have never learned how to say it effectively. There are many men who have truth to teach, but who have never succeded in teaching it, because they never learned the technique and the method of teaching. Let no man despise the study of the technique of teaching! Jesus did not despise it. Jesus had something to say and he knew how to say it, and the teacher will still find in him the perfect model.

11

WHAT JESUS SAID ABOUT GOD

The distinguishing and differentiating characteristic of the message of Jesus is that it is a *gospel*. The word 'gospel' *(euaggelion)* means good news, and it was good news that Jesus came to bring. No one could have called the message of John the Baptizer good news: it was the message of a threat with the axe poised at the root of the tree, the fire about to descend, judgment and destruction to be launched upon the world. It was good news of great joy that the angelic host brought to the shepherds as they watched their flocks by night (Luke 2.10). Mark's title for his book is 'the beginning of the gospel of Jesus Christ' (Mark 1.1). It was to announce good news to the poor that Jesus came (Luke 4.18; 7.22). It was the good news of the Kingdom that he brought to men in the synagogue, in the open places, in the towns and villages, and in the Temple (Matt. 4.23; 9.35; Luke 8.1; 20.1). It was his initial summons to men that they should repent and believe the good news (Mark 1.14f.), and, when he sent out his twelve men, it was with good news that he sent them (Luke 9.6). Jesus' message to men is good news about God.

If, then, Jesus came to bring good news about God, it must mean that he came to tell men things about God that they did not know, or did not realize, before. We must therefore begin by examining the beliefs of men about God before Jesus came.

The Jewish conception of God can be summed up in one word, the word 'holy'. Again and again God is described as 'The Holy One of Israel' (II Kings 19.22; Ps. 89.18; Isa. 1.4; 5.24; 10.20; 30.11; 47.4; 60.9; Jer. 50.29; Hos. 11.9). In Isaiah alone God is described as 'The Holy One' no fewer than twenty-nine times. Again and again in the law a law is laid down as binding and obligatory because it is given by the God who is 'holy' (Lev. 19.2; 20.26; 21.8). God must be given exclusive service because he is a holy God (Josh. 24.19). In Hannah's prayer there is none as holy as the Lord (I Sam. 2.2). God, says the Psalmist, must be exalted because he is holy (Ps. 99.9). As Isaiah heard it, the cry of the seraphim is: 'Holy, holy, holy is the Lord of hosts' (Isa. 6.3). The holiness of God is the primary doctrine of Judaism.

In Hebrew the word for 'holy' is *qadosh*, which has as its root meaning 'different', 'separate', 'set apart'. The thing or the person described as holy is different, separate, set apart from other things or persons. The priest is holy because he is different from other men; the Temple is holy because it is different from other buildings; the Sabbath day is holy because it is different from other days. God is supremely holy because he is different from all other persons and beings; he belongs to a different scale and sphere of life; he is completely different from men; he is the 'wholly other', the one who is essentially different from men. Inevitably this conception, whose key-note is difference, has certain consequences.

(i) It issues in the conception of *the unapproachability of God*. Clearly the difference between God and man sets a vast and unbridgeable gulf between God and man. But to Jewish thought it did more than that. God is so different from men that to approach God at all is dangerous and even fatal. No man can enter into the nearer presence of God and escape with his life.

After the wrestling at Peniel, it is Jacob's astonished and incredulous cry: 'I have seen God face to face, and yet my life is preserved' (Gen. 32.30). As Moses heard it, God said to him: 'You cannot see my face; for man shall not see me and live' (Ex. 33.20). When Gideon realized who his visitor had been, he cried out in terror: 'Alas, O Lord God! For now I have seen the angel of the Lord face to face.' And God's answer was: 'Peace be to you; do not fear; you shall not die' (Judg. 6.22f.). When Manoah discovered that the messenger who had brought him news of the coming birth of a son was an angel of the Lord, his terrified reaction was: 'We shall surely die, for we have seen God' (Judg. 13.22). At this stage of things the idea is that God is so holy, so different, so unapproachable, that to see him is to die.

This essential difference between God and man is called *the transcendence of God;* and with the course of the centuries this idea of the transcendence of God was not lessened but intensified. In the Old Testament story of the giving of the law, the law was given to Moses directly from God. The people were amazed that God had that day talked with a man and that that man was still alive (Deut. 5.24). But twice in the New Testament we are told that that the law was given, not directly from God, but through angelic intermediaries (Acts 7.53; Gal. 3.18). By New Testament times the idea was that God was so different and separate and apart from men, so transcendent, that any transaction between God and men could not be direct, but must be performed through some intermediary.

So, then, the idea of the holiness of God issued in the idea of the dangerous unapproachability of God. H. G. Wells in one of his novels tells of a man, near to mental and spiritual collapse under the stress and strain of things, who was told by his nerve specialist that his only hope lay in fellowship with God. The man's amazed answer was that he would as soon think of cooling his throat with the milky way or shaking hands with the stars as having fellowship with God. That is a parallel to the orthodox Jewish idea of God.

(ii) This idea of the holiness of God issues in the idea of what might be called *the unpredictability of God*. It is difficult to put this idea into actual words. In the Old Testament God is *King* far more than he is *Father*. In the ancient world the king was an absolute monarch, answerable and responsible to no one. Suetonius tells us how Caligula, the Roman Emperor, told his grandmother to remember that he could do anything he liked and do it to anyone. The idea is that in the presence of God man has no rights whatever, that there is no reason whatever why man should understand, or see any reason in, the acts of God as they affect either himself or the world.

There are two Old Testament passages which illustrate this absolute power of God. The first is Jeremiah's parable of the potter and the clay (Jer. 18.1-10). Jeremiah sees the potter work with the clay; it does not come off his wheel in the way in which the potter wants it to; he simply crushes it down and begins all over again. Then Jeremiah hears God say: 'O house of Israel, can I not do with you as this potter has done? Behold, like the clay in the potter's hand, so are you in mine hand, O house of

Israel.' The more one thinks of that passage the more terrible it becomes. Men have no more rights in the presence of God than the clay in the hands of the potter; men have no more right to understand than the clay; God can take and make and break living, human personalities as the potter can take and make and break the clay.

The second passage is in Job 38 and 39. Job, the good man, is involved in disaster; he would state his case to God; and in these chapters is God's answer to him. From the point of view of magnificent and dramatic poetry they rank with the great literature of the world—but they are terrible chapters. 'Where were you when I laid the foundation of the earth? . . . Have you entered into the springs of the sea? . . . Have the gates of death been revealed to you? . . . Have you comprehended the expanse of the earth? . . . Do you know the ordinances of the heavens? . . . Can you send forth lightnings?' On and on goes this battery and bombardment of unanswerable questions, the whole essence of which is that God is saying: 'What right have you to speak to me? Who are you to claim to understand what I do? I am not answerable and responsible to you. My power and holiness give me the right to do as I like—even to smash you.' It is magnificent—but it is cold comfort for an agonized body and a broken heart. Here is the picture of the unpredictable God, the God whom a man cannot understand and is not meant to understand, the God before whom a man can only bow his head with all resistance broken.

(iii)   Inevitably this idea of the holiness of God leads to another idea about God. God's holiness will necessarily affect his relationship with all men, but it is bound very specially to affect his relationship with the sinner. There are in the Old Testament voices, such as the voice of Hosea, which speak from hearts which have glimpsed the patient love and the infinite mercy of God; but in the main stream of Jewish orthodox thought God is the God whose aim is the destruction of the sinner.

'Let sinners be consumed from the earth,' says the Psalmist, 'and let the wicked be no more!' (Ps. 104.35). 'Rebels and sinners shall be destroyed together,' writes Isaiah, 'and those who forsake the Lord shall be consumed' (Isa. 1.28). 'The day of the Lord comes, cruel, with wrath and fierce anger, to make the earth a desolation, and to destroy its sinners from it' (Isa. 13.9). 'All the sinners of my people,' Amos hears God say, 'shall die by the sword' (Amos 9.10). There is a rabbinic saying: 'There is joy before God when those who provoke him perish from the world.' The holy God is set on the destruction of the sinner.

Nowhere does this appear more vividly than in the words of Ps. 24. 'Who shall ascend the hill of the Lord? And who shall stand in his holy place? He who has clean hands and a pure heart; who does not lift up his soul to what is false and does not swear deceitfully. He will receive blessing from the Lord and vindication from the God of his salvation' (Ps. 24.3-5). That is often read at the beginning of a Christian service, and yet to any sensitive and thinking man the effect of it is to slam the door to God's presence in his face. This is the Jewish conception which thought of the holy God as absolutely hostile to sinners, and which filled the scribes and Pharisees with horror, when they saw Jesus eating with and befriending and companying with tax-gatherers and sinners.

Judaism stressed the holiness of God. That holiness stretched a great gulf between God and man; it surrounded God with a certain sublime unpredictability without any responsibility to men; it tended to make men think of God as the sworn enemy of the sinner.

Before very long in its history Christianity was to go out to the Greek and Roman world. What ideas of God would the Christian message encounter there? Would the Christian message of God be good news about God there also? What were the Greek and Roman ideas about God and about the gods?

(i) The oldest, the most primitive, and perhaps the commonest idea was the idea of *grudging gods*. There was an essential hostility and suspicion between gods and men. The gods grudged men everything they attained, achieved, or received. To be successful, prosperous or great was dangerous; mediocrity alone was safe. Herodotus found a parable in the fact that the tallest trees were most likely to be blasted by the lightning stroke; any man who raised himself out of the common ruck of men was in danger of being blasted by the gods.

The typical story is the story of Prometheus. Prometheus cared for men. He therefore stole fire from heaven, gave it to men, and taught them how to use it. Zeus, chief of the gods, was mightily angry. He caused Prometheus to be chained to a rock in Scythia; he prepared a vulture to tear out Prometheus' liver every day, which ever grew again only to be torn out again, until in the end Hercules freed him from his torture.

Here is the essence of the matter. The gods were enraged that men should enter into any blessing. Man was not the child of the gods; he was rather the victim of the gods. There was an essential conflict of interests, an essential enmity between gods and men.

(ii) The gods were *the unknown and the unknowable gods*. It is true that in the great days of Greek thought men believed that the power of human thought could scale the heights of heaven and storm the citadels of the divine. But even then the discoveries could only be for the few, the very few. As Plato had it, it is difficult to find out about God, and when you have found out about him, it is impossible to tell anyone else about him. Discovery is difficult, communication impossible. Even the greatest men, as Plutarch had it, only see God when they have removed themselves from the body, and then only like a flash of light in thick darkness—a moment of illumination, and then the dark again. Never God and man can meet, as Plato said. 'To whom, then,' said Plutarch, 'shall I recite prayers? To whom tender vows? To whom slay victims? To whom shall I call to help the wretched, to favour the good, to counter the evil?' The gods were beyond the reach of men.

(iii) To the Greeks the gods were *detached from the world*. The actual government of the world was in the hands of the *daimons*, who were intermediaries between gods and men. The *daimons* were in charge of the natural forces and the day-to-day ordering of the world and its ways and affairs. As Glover put it: 'The One God is by common consent far from all direct contact with this or any other universe of becoming and perishing.' 'The Ultimate God rules through deputies,' but is himself completely detached from the world. If you remove the *daimons*, Plutarch held, you make confusion and disorder of everything, 'bringing God in among mortal passions and mortal affairs, fetching him down for our needs.' 'He who involves God in human needs does not spare his majesty, nor does he maintain the dignity and greatness of God's excellence.' The *daimons* are everywhere but God is nowhere among men. The idea of an incarnation would have been incredible to a Greek.

(iv) All this came to a head in the two great philosophies which were the religion of the world in New Testament times. These two great philosophies were Epicureanism and Stoicism. For the Epicurean the gods were beings without a care. For the Epicurean the end of life was *ataraxia,* absolute untroubled serenity, absence of pain of body and trouble of mind. The gods alone enjoy *ataraxia* in perfection, and, since that is so, they are bound to be completely detached from the world. If they were in the least interested in the world, if they were in the least involved in the world, it would mean that they were bound to know worry, anxiety, effort, care. The first sentence in the *Principal Doctrines* of Epicurus is: 'The blessed and immortal nature knows no trouble itself nor causes trouble to any other, so that it is never constrained by anger or favour. For all such things exist only in the weak.' Lucretius describes the gods: 'The very nature of divinity must necessarily enjoy immortal life in the deepest peace, far removed and separated from our troubles; for without any pain, without danger, itself mighty by its own resources, needing us not at all, it is neither propitiated with services, nor touched by wrath.' So the gods live in their remote majesty in 'their peaceful abodes, which no winds ever shake nor clouds besprinkle with rain, which no snow congealed by the bitter frost mars, but the air ever cloudless encompasses them and laughs with its light spread wide abroad. There moreover nature supplies everything, and nothing at any time impairs their peace of mind.'[1] It was thus that Tennyson, in 'The Lotos Eaters', drew his picture of the gods:

> For they lie beside their nectar, and the bolts are hurl'd
> Far below them in the valleys, and the clouds are lightly curl'd
> Round their golden houses, girdled with the gleaming world:
> Where they smile in secret, looking over wasted lands,
> Blight and famine, plague and earthquake, roaring deeps and
> fiery sands,
> Clanging fights, and flaming towns, and sinking ships, and
> praying hands.

[1] Lucretius 1.646ff.; 3.18ff.

This is the conception, not of gods who are hostile to men, but of gods who, because they are gods, are completely unaware of the existence of man and of the world.

The other great philosophy of the Greek world in the age to which the Christian message came was Stoicism. The aim of the Stoics was to attain perfect tranquillity, *eudaimonia,* a happiness which is perfect peace. A state of perfect peace is a state in which a man lives a life in which there is no such thing as an unsatisfied desire. Therefore, the way to happiness in life is to eliminate deliberately every desire. Teach yourself to be absolutely indifferent, to desire nothing. Not only must we desire *nothing;* we must also desire *no one.* As Edwyn Bevan put it: 'Leave one small hole in a ship's side and you let in the sea. The Stoics, I think, saw with perfect truth that if you were going to allow any least entrance of love and pity into the breast, you admitted something whose measure you could not control, and might just as well give up the idea of inner tranquillity at once.' To attain tranquillity, said the Stoic, you must banish all emotion for ever and ever.

If that be true of men, it is still truer of God. If anyone can feel love and pity, it means that some one else can have some influence over him; it means that some one else can make him sad or glad. Now, if some one else can make us sad or glad, it means that for the moment that person can influence us, has power over us, and is greater than we are. Clearly no one can be greater than God; that means that no one can ever influence God; that must mean that no one can ever make God sad or glad; no one can move the feelings and emotions of God, or that person would be, if only momentarily, greater than God. Therefore the first essential in God is that he must be totally without feeling; he cannot feel love or pity and remain God. The first and essential attribute of God is what the Stoics called *apatheia,* which is not apathy in the sense of indifference, but apathy in the sense of absolute incapability of all feeling.

To the Stoics God was *the God without a heart,* the God who could not care, the God to whom pity and love were utterly impossible, just because he was God. In Epicureanism men are confronted with gods who are not even aware of their existence; in Stoicism men are confronted with a God who, because he is

God, cannot care; and it is hard to say which is worse for wounded hearts.

We must now go on to see the good news about God which Jesus brought, and with which Christianity went out to meet the human situation. To begin with, two things immediately stand out.

The fact that Jesus came is the proof that God is *a self-revealing God*. The coming of Jesus is the proof that God is not the hidden and the unknowable God, but that his great desire is to be known by men. Further, this knowledge of God is not open only to the few, the philosopher, the theologian, the man of high intellectual stature and of great intellectual calibre. It is open to all, even to the simplest. The reason for this is that it is a knowledge which is based on love. Here is the difference between *knowing* a person and *knowing about* a person. *To know about* a person is an exercise of the mind, and such knowledge may be achieved without ever having met the person at all. For instance, we *know about* the great figures of past history, and we *know about* the great figures of the present day who move in a circle and a sphere into which we are never likely to penetrate. *To know* a person is essentially an exercise of the heart, and a personal relationship. We cannot really *know* either a person or a subject unless we love that person or that subject.

It is perfectly true that there are many questions about God, man, and the world, to answer which requires the most strenuous efforts of the greatest minds and the highest intellects. The systematization of Christian truth certainly requires the toil and labour of the mind. But to know God personally as companion, friend and lover of the souls of men is a knowledge which is open to all.

Paul Tournier, the great Christian doctor, declares that life, in order to be life, must necessarily be *dialogue*. No one can find life in any real sense of the term in isolation. He must find it in contact, in dialogue, with others. The supreme dialogue of life is the dialogue with God. Paul Tournier writes: 'Jesus Christ is the dialogue re-established. He is God coming to us because we cannot go to him.' Jesus came with the good news that God is not a God who hides himself, that God is not a God whom only the philosophers may know, that God is the God who at all costs desires to be known, and who in the most costly way has revealed himself to all men.

The second general fact which stands out in the message which Jesus brought is that *God is involved in the human situation*. It was precisely this that both Jew and Greek had come to deny. The Jews so stressed the holiness and the transcendence of God that they removed him from human contact altogether. They even, in popular thought, delegated to the archangels the duty of presenting the prayers of the faithful to God. Sometimes that was held to be the duty of Michael, sometimes of Raphael. 'I am Raphael,' says Raphael to Tobit, 'one of the seven holy angels, who present the prayers of the saints and enter into the presence of the glory of the Holy One' (Tobit 12.15). The Greeks considered it an insult to God, a complete misunderstanding of the nature and the being of God, to involve God in the world or in the human situation at all. The entry of Jesus into the world is the proof that God is involved in, identified with, the human situation. In Jesus the God who was afar off has indeed been brought near.

There is a third great fact about the Jewish and the Greek idea of God which includes the other two. Both the Jews and the Greeks really believed in a God who is essentially *a selfish God*. It is for the sake of the glory of God that sinners must be destroyed; the supremacy of God will brook no rival and no disobedience. The serenity and the tranquillity of the gods are all that matter; anything that would even tend to affect the peace of the gods must be eliminated. The idea of the pain and the sorrow of God is far removed from all that. But Jesus brought into the world the message of *a selfless God,* a God to whom men were so dear that he bore their sins and sorrows on his heart, and gave himself for them. It may be drawing the contrast too violently, but there is a certain truth in saying that before Jesus came men thought of a God who existed and ordered all things for his own sake; after Jesus came men were given the vision of a God who existed and ordered all things for the sake of men. The God of Jesus is love—and love is always selfless, when it is true love.

So Jesus came to men, and the Christian Church went out to

the world, with the message of a self-revealing God, a God who is involved in the human situation, a God who is selfless in his love for men. It is from these great facts about God that everything else follows.

(i) Jesus came to tell men of an *inviting* God, a God who desires to be approached. One of the great characteristic words of Jesus is the word 'Come!'. He invited men to follow him in discipleship (Mark 1.17; Matt. 4.19). He invited his own men to share his solitary prayer and communion with God (Mark 6.31). He invited the weary and the heavy-laden to come to him for rest and help (Matt. 11.28). He likened his own invitation to the invitation to a marriage feast (Matt. 22.4). He told in his parable of how, in the days to come, those who cared as he cared would be invited to share the glory that was prepared for them (Matt. 25.34). Continually on Jesus' lips there was an invitation.

It is difficult to imagine anyone holding an intimate and loving conversation with one of the Greek gods, or even with the holy God of the Old Testament; but, for the Christian, God is the God with an eternal invitation in his heart, and prayer is the acceptance of that invitation to speak with, and to listen to, God. H. V. Morton in *A Traveller in Rome* tells of a scene he watched in the Church of St Clemente. A poor, old, ragged woman, like a little black ghost, came shuffling in in carpet slippers. 'She was like a bundle of old, dry leaves wrapped round with cobweb. First she knelt and told her beads, then she approached the crucifix, and, bending forward, kissed the feet, and placed her cheek against them, whispering all the time . . . She seemed to be holding a conversation with the crucifix, pausing as if for a reply, and then speaking again . . . I fancied from her manner that she was in the habit of talking to Christ like this, perhaps telling him her anxieties, and maybe the events in the tenement where she lived.' Here was a simple person conversing with God. It is the invitation to do that that Jesus brought.

The Synoptic Gospels all say that, at the moment Jesus died, the veil which shut off the Holy of Holies in the Temple was rent in two (Matt. 27.51; Mark 15.38; Luke 23.45). Into the Holy of Holies only one man could enter, and that only on one day in the year. Into the Holy of Holies only the High Priest could enter, and the one day on which he could enter was the

Day of Atonement; and even on that day the time during which he might linger in the Holy of Holies was strictly limited. The instruction was that he must linger no longer than necessary, lest he put Israel in terror, and lest the people fear that God had smitten him dead. The rending of the veil is the symbolic statement of the fact that Jesus came to men with an invitation to approach the God to whose presence there were no barriers any more. Once it had been the belief that to see God is to die; Jesus came with the invitation to all men to enter into the presence of God with childlike confidence and boldness.

(ii)   This invitation was not only an invitation to those who, as it were, deserved it, to those who were morally good, spiritually devout, perfectly righteous. It was an invitation to sinners, for Jesus came with the message of a *forgiving* God. Around him the taxgatherers and the sinners and the women of the streets gathered (Luke 15.1). He ate with them (Matt. 9.10; Mark 2.15; Luke 5.30), so that the righteous orthodox of his day called him the friend of publicans and sinners (Matt. 11.19; Luke 7.34). He said that he had come to call, not the righteous, but sinners to repentance (Matt. 9.13; Mark 2.17; Luke 5.32), and that he had come to seek and to save that which was lost (Matt. 18.11). He said that there was joy in heaven over one sinner who repents (Luke 15.7,10).

There is a world of difference here. The Pharisees and the orthodox Jews who kept the law avoided sinners as they avoided people with the plague. People who knew that they were sinners would never have dared to approach the scribes and the Pharisees, even if they had wished to. This is a far cry from the God who can only be approached by those who have clean hands and a pure heart (Ps. 24.4), and whose aim it is to obliterate the sinner.

Jesus came with the message of a God whose love not even sin could destroy, and whose heart's desire was that men should accept the offer of forgiveness which he was making to them, and, in being forgiven, should learn to mend their ways.

(iii)   Jesus came with news of God even more startling than that God was an inviting and a forgiving God. The Jew would not have doubted that, if a sinner came creeping back to God in remorse, contrition and repentance, and if he humbly pleaded for forgiveness, he would be forgiven. God would accept the man who came humbly and penitently back to him. But Jesus came to tell of a *seeking God,* a God who did not wait for the sinner to come back, but who went out to seek and to search for him, and to appeal to him to come back.

This is the fact about Jesus which above all impressed C. G. Montefiore, the great Jewish liberal scholar. Again and again in his commentary on the Synoptic Gospels he returns to this idea of the seeking God as to something which was absolutely new. Commenting on Mark 2.17 he writes: 'Jesus sought to bring back into glad communion with God those whom sin, whether "moral" or "ceremonial" had driven away. For him sinners (at least certain types of sinners) were the subject not of condemnation or disdain, but of pity. He did not avoid sinners, but sought them out. They were still children of God. This was a new and sublime contribution to the development of religion and morality . . . To deny the greatness and originality of Jesus in this connection, to deny that he opened a new chapter in men's attitude to sin and sinners, is, I think, to beat the head against the wall.' Again, in commenting on Matt. 9.36, he writes: 'So far as we can tell, this pity for the sinner was a new note in religious history.' Again on Luke 15.1 he writes: 'The sinners drew near to hear him. Surely this is a new note, something which we have not yet heard in the Old Testament, or of its heroes, something we have not heard in the *Talmud,* or of its heroes. "The sinners drew near to hear him." His teaching did not repel them. It did not palter with, or make light of, sin, but yet it gave comfort to the sinner. The virtues of repentance are gloriously praised in the Rabbinical literature, but this direct search for, and appeal to the sinner are new and moving notes of high import and significance. The good shepherd who searches for the lost sheep and reclaims it, and rejoices over it, is a new figure which has never ceased to play its great part in the moral and religious development of the world.' Montefiore stresses the newness of the human side of this. In commenting on Matt. 18.10-14 he writes: 'What is new and striking in the teaching of Jesus is that this process of repentance takes an active turn. Man is bidden not merely to receive the penitent gladly, but to seek out the sinner, to try to redeem him, to make him penitent.'

To Montefiore the idea of the seeking God, the God pictured in terms of a woman seeking a lost coin, and a shepherd seeking a lost sheep (Luke 15.1-10) was something quite unparallelled and gloriously new.

It would be great if God accepted us back when we came to him in humble penitence; it would be precious that God should wait for the sinner to come back. But that God should go out and seek the sinner is something sublime, and something new. Here, indeed, is good news of God.

(iv)   This truth of the seeking God has a necessary corollary. God is the God of *the individual love*. It is not *mankind* that God loves; it is *men*. The shepherd cannot be content with ninety-nine sheep while one is lost; the woman cannot be content with nine coins while one is lost; the one, the individual, matters intensely to God.

Paul Tournier is fascinated by what he calls the *personalism* of the Bible. God says to Moses: 'I know you *by name*' (Ex. 33.17). God says through Isaiah: 'It is I, the Lord, who call you by name' (Isa. 45.3). Paul Tournier tells of a girl who was one of his patients. She was the youngest daughter in a large family, the support of which was a sore problem to the father. One day she heard him mutter despairingly, referring to her: 'We could well have done without that one!' That is precisely what no one will ever hear God say. The love of God is at one and the same time completely universal and completely individual. As Augustine so beautifully expressed it: 'God loves each one of us as if there was only one of us to love.' With God there is no one who is lost in the crowd.

There is a saying of Jesus which appears in two forms and the variation in it may be the symbol of this individual love of God. Matthew reports Jesus as saying: 'Are not two sparrows sold for a farthing? And one of them shall not fall on the ground without your Father's will' (Matt. 10.29). Luke reports Jesus as saying: 'Are not five sparrows sold for two farthings? And not one of them is forgotten before God' (Luke 12.6). Jesus in all probability used both forms of the saying, and used them both at the same time. If a purchaser was prepared to spend one farthing, he received two sparrows; but, if he was prepared to spend two farthings, he received not four sparrows, but five, for one was thrown into the bargain, as if it was worth nothing at all. Not even the sparrow which in human eyes has no value at all is forgotten by God.

Even the individual who on human valuation is valueless is valuable to God. It is easy to see what such message must have meant to the slaves of the Empire who were defined by law not as persons but as living tools, with no more rights than a tool.

(v) It may be that we dare to go on to something further yet. Other thinkers have called God by various names—The Supreme God, The First Cause, The Creative Energy, The Life Force. All these descriptions of God have one characteristic in common—they are *impersonal*. But Jesus always spoke and taught of a God who is a *person*. In all reverence we may draw a certain conclusion from that. No person can exist in isolation; personality and isolation are mutually contradictory. Every person needs other persons to complete himself. It is in communication and fellowship with other persons that personality is fulfilled and realized. We therefore come to the astonishing conclusion that *God needs men*; that in some mysterious sense creation was for God a necessity; that somehow God needs the world and men to complete himself. That is why God created men and the world; that is why God loves men with an everlasting love; and that is why God would go to any lengths of sacrifice to bring men back to himself.

A negro poet, James Weldon Johnson, has put the matter in the way in which a child might put it. His poem is not theology—theology might well be shocked by it—but it has a childlike truth.

> And God stepped out on space,
> And he looked around, and said:
> 'I'm lonely—
> I'll make me a world.'
>
> Then God walked around,
> And God looked around
> On all that he had made.
> He looked at his sun,
> And he looked at his moon,
> And he looked at his little stars;

He looked on his world
With all its living things,
And God said: 'I'm lonely still.'
Then God sat down—
On the side of a hill where he could think,
By a deep, wide river he sat down,
With his head in his hands,
God thought and thought,
Till he thought: 'I'll make me a man.'

There is a child's truth there, the truth that God needs man, because God is a person; and from that need there springs the forgiving, seeking, individual love of God. But that is something of which no one had dreamed till Jesus brought to men the good news of God.

. All that Jesus came to say about God is summed up in the name by which he himself called God, and by which he taught others to call God, the name *Father*. The name Father as applied to God had a long history before Jesus came to give it a new meaning and a new content, for Jesus was by no means the first to call God Father.

The word 'father' can have behind it two spheres of meaning. It can be connected either with *paternity* or with *fatherhood*. When the word 'father' is connected with the idea of paternity, it means no more than the person who gave a child life, who begat him, who brought him into this world. It is perfectly possible that a father in this sense may never even set eyes on his child. The sole relationship between father and child in this sense of the term is the relationship of physical begetting, and father and child could live their lives and go through the world and never even meet. In the idea of paternity there is no necessary intimacy, fellowship, love. On the other hand when the word father is connected with the idea of fatherhood, it describes a relationship of closeness and intimacy and love. It describes a relationship in which day by day, so long as life and need last, the father cares for the child in body, mind and spirit, in which the father nourishes the child with food, guides the child with advice, surrounds and strengthens the child with continual love.

It was not until the coming of Jesus that men learned the full meaning of the fatherhood of God, although for many centuries they had been groping their way to it.

(i)   Men began with the idea of God as father in the sense of *the progenitor of their race*. That is to say, they thought of the fatherhood of God in terms of paternity. It was he who had begotten their race, and it was to him that they owed their lives in the physical sense of the term. So we find Syrian names like Abibaal, which means son of Baal, and Benhadad, which means son of Hadad; Baal and Hadad were Syrian gods. So we find a tribe calling themselves 'sons of Hobal', and Hobal was their god. So we find the Greeks calling Zeus 'Father of gods and men', and meaning much what a modern man would mean, if he called God 'The First Cause', or 'The Life Force'. In this idea there is little or no thought of intimacy or fellowship; the idea is that of God as father in the sense of the physical giver of life.

(ii)   The Jews had always a vivid sense of God as *the father of their nation*. So they can say:

'Do you thus requite the Lord,
you foolish and senseless people?
Is not he your father, who created you,
who made you and established you?' (Deut. 32.6).

'Have we not all one father?
Has not one God created us?
Why then are ye faithless to one another?' (Mal. 2.10).

At this stage there is a definite conviction that God is the father and founder and possessor of the nation, but so far the fatherhood of God is to the nation, not to the individual within it.

(iii)   There is one exception to this. If God is the father of the nation, then it is not unnatural that in a special sense he may be called *the father of the king of the nation*. The promise of God to David regarding David's son is: 'I will be his father, and he shall be my son' (II Sam. 7.14). The coronation psalm says of the king: 'You are my son, today I have begotten you' (Ps. 2.7). But this very psalm shows that the sonship comes to the king as king; it is on the day that he becomes king that he becomes son. God becomes the king's father, not because the king is an individual man, but because the nation is personified and embodied in him. We have not yet reached a stage at which God is thought of as the father of the individual.

(iv)　The nation of Israel is in a very special sense the child of God, and God is in a very special sense the father of Israel. God is the father of Israel in a sense in which he is not the father of any other nation. This must mean that *God has become the father of Israel by a special act of choice and of adoption.* Jeremiah hears God say: 'I am a father to Israel, and Ephraim is my firstborn' (Jer. 31.9). Choice and adoption require some moment when the choice is made and when the adoption becomes effective. Very often the Jews saw the special adoption by God of their nation in the deliverance from Egypt. Then God stepped in, and in a special sense made Israel his nation. Hosea hears God say: 'When Israel was a child, I loved him, and out of Egypt I called my son' (Hos. 11.1). God's message through Moses to Pharaoh was: 'Israel is my firstborn son, and I say to you, "Let my son go that he may serve me" ' (Ex. 4.22). Once this act of choice and adoption had been made, it was carried out, confirmed and cemented in the events of history as they affected Israel for weal or for woe. In the wilderness Israel has seen 'how the Lord your God bore you, as a man bears his son' (Deut. 1.31). 'As a man disciplines his son, the Lord your God disciplines you' (Deut. 8.5). Isaiah hears God say: 'Sons have I reared and brought up, but they have rebelled against me' (Isa. 1.2). Still at this stage it is the nation which is in question, and God is not yet the father of the individual.

(v)　But out of this stage there emerges a very important development. Any act of choice, any act of adoption, by the very fact that it is made, automatically demands a response. Quite clearly, all Israel has not made that response to God; many have been deaf to God's commands and have turned their backs on God's appeal. Only some have responded in love and in obedience to the choice and the adoption of God. It, therefore, follows that *God is the father of the good and of the righteous in a way in which he cannot be the father of the disobedient and the rebellious.* Often the commandments of God run like this: 'You are the sons of the Lord your God; therefore you shall not . . .' (e.g. Deut. 14.1). Sonship and obedience must go together. 'A son honours his father, and a servant his master. If then I am a father, where is my honour?' (Mal. 1.6). 'As a father pities his children, so the Lord pities *those who fear him*' (Ps. 103.13). Here we are at the first great step towards the individualizing of the fatherhood of God. The nation is still God's nation; but there is a quite different relationship between God and the obedient from that which exists between God and the rebellious.

(vi)   Another way in which to express this is to say that man's sonship of God becomes *an ethical sonship*. This is an idea which gains strength all through the literature between the Testaments. In *Jubilees* God says: 'Their souls shall cleave to me and to all my commandments, and they will fulfil my commandments, and I will be their father and they will be my children' (*Jubilees* 1.24). 'He correcteth the righteous as a beloved son' (*Psalms of Solomon* 13.8). There is a rabbinic saying: 'Be strong as a leopard and swift as an eagle and fleet as a gazelle and brave as a lion to do the will of your father who is in heaven.'

There was within the Jewish nation a not unnatural reaction to this. An ethical sonship makes great demands on a man; it demands his love, his loyalty, his devotion, his obedience. There were Jews who insisted that God was so much the father of the nation of Israel that any Israelite was safe from all judgment simply because he was a son of Abraham, which indeed was the view that John the Baptizer attacked (Luke 3.8). 'A single Israelite,' says the *Talmud*, 'is worth more in God's sight than all the nations of the world.' Justin charges the Jewish teachers with teaching that an Israelite, just because he is of the seed of Abraham, will receive the Kingdom even if he is a sinner, faithless and disobedient.[1]

It is quite true that there was in not a few cases this degeneration of the idea of the fatherhood of God, but in the highest and the best Jewish thought the idea of sonship was acquiring an increasingly ethical quality, and that fact made the individualizing of the fatherhood of God an increasing reality.

(vii)   Once a man realizes that true sonship and devoted and loving obedience go hand in hand, then the note of a personal, individual relationship enters in. True, the individualizing of

[1]   *Dialogue with Trypho* 140.

the fatherhood of God is not yet common, but the Sage in his difficulties can pray: 'Lord, Father, and Master of my life' (Ecclus 23.1). There the true individual note strikes.

Because of this there enters into Jewish thought, at least on rare occasions, a new tenderness and intimacy in the relationship between God and man. G. F. Moore in *Judaism* quotes a beautiful comment on Ex. 14.19 by Rabbi Judas ben Ila'i: 'The angel of God who went before the camp removed and went behind them. It is like a man who was walking in the way, and letting his son go on before him. Came robbers in front to take the boy captive, the father put him behind him. Came a wolf from behind, he put him in front. Came robbers in front, and wolves behind, he took him up in his arms. Did he begin to be troubled by the heat of the sun, his father stretched his garment over him. Was he hungry, he gave him food; thirsty, he gave him drink. Just so God did.'

Stage by stage, the individualizing of the idea of the fatherhood of God was coming about; and yet it had a long, long way to go before there could come into it the tenderness, the intimacy, the childlike confidence which Jesus was to bring.

(viii) When we come finally to examine Jesus' conception of the fatherhood of God, we meet with two most significant and illuminating facts.

(*a*) There is the *extraordinary rarity* with which Jesus uses the name 'Father', as applied to God, at all. In Mark, the earliest of the Gospels, Jesus only calls God 'Father' four times (Mark 8.38; 11.25; 13.32; 14.36). Further, in Mark Jesus does not call God 'Father' at all until after Peter's confession at Caesarea Philippi, and then he only does so within the circle of the disciples. There is only one conclusion to be drawn from this. To Jesus, to call God Father was no theological commonplace; it was something so sacred that he could hardly speak of it at all in public; and, when he did speak of it, it was only in the presence of those who, at least to some extent, understood.

(*b*) There is the *extraordinary intimacy* which Jesus put into the term. Jesus called God '*Abba*, Father' (Mark 14.36). As Jeremias points out there is not even the remotest parallel to this in all Jewish literature. *Abba*, like the modern Arabic *jaba*, is the word used by a young child to his father. It is the ordinary, everyday family word which a little child used in speaking to his father.[1] It is completely untranslatable. Any attempt to put it into English ends in bathos or grotesqueness. It is a word which no one had ever ventured to use in addressing God before.

For Jesus the fatherhood of God was something of almost inexpressible sacredness, and it was something of unsurpassable tender intimacy. In it is summed up everything that he came to say about God in his relationship with men.

When we set this conception of God as the Father, to whom a man may go with the same confidence and trust as a child goes to his earthly father, beside the Jewish conception of the remote transcendence of God and beside the Greek conceptions of the grudging God, the gods who are unaware of our existence, the god without a heart, we see that it is indeed true that Jesus brought to men good news about God.

[1] *The Parables of Jesus,* p. 134.

12

WHAT JESUS SAID ABOUT MAN AND SIN

I T is not possible to move far amidst the sayings and the writings of the serious minds of any age without coming upon the essential paradox of manhood. On the one side we come upon passage after passage which speaks of the futility, the helplessness, the degradation, the degeneration, the sin of life. 'Men,' said Seneca, 'love their vices and hate them at the same time.'[1] 'The beginning of philosophy,' he says, 'is a consciousness of one's weakness in necessary things.' Man oscillates between right and wrong, unable to declare boldly and unequivocally for either. Glover summarizes the letter of Serenus to Seneca: 'I find myself not quite free, nor yet quite in bondage to the faults which I feared and hated. I am in a state, not the worst indeed, but very querulous and uncomfortable, neither well nor ill. It is a weakness of the mind that sways between the two, that will neither bravely turn to right nor to wrong. Things disturb me, though they do not alter my principles. I think of public life; something worries me, and I fall back into the life of leisure, to be pricked to the will to act by reading some brave words, or seeing some fine example. I beg you, if you have any remedy to stay my fluctuation of mind, count me worthy to owe you peace. To put what I endure into a simile, it is not the tempest that troubles me, but sea-sickness.'[2]

Sometimes the matter is worse than wavering oscillation; it is utter moral helplessness. Let the guilty see virtue, says Persius, and mourn that they have lost her for ever.[3] He speaks of filthy Natta 'benumbed by vice'. Epictetus demands: 'When a man is hardened like a stone, how shall we be able to deal with him by argument?' Here is the picture of the man who, as Glover put it, is suffering from necrosis of the soul. Seneca can call himself *homo non tolerabilis,* a man not to be tolerated.[4] Marcus Aurelius

1 *Letters* 112.3.
2 *Concerning Tranquillity of Mind* 1.
3 *Satires* 3.38.
4 *Letters* 57.3.

can speak with a kind of contempt for manhood: 'Of man's life, his time is a point, his existence a flux, his sensation clouded, his body's entire composition corruptible, his vital spirit an eddy of breath, his fortune hard to predict, his fame uncertain. Briefly, all the things of the body are a river; all the things of the spirit, dream and delirium' (2.17).

On the one side there are the voices of pessimism, of help-lessness, and of despair. But on the other side, often in the very same writers, there emerges at least in flashes the conviction of the greatness of man. The same Seneca, who is so conscious of frustation and of sin, can write: 'God is near you, with you, within you. I say it, Lucilius; a holy spirit sits within us, spectator of our evil and our good, our guardian.'[1] Glover collects certain of the things which Epictetus in his *Discourses* says of man. Man's part in life is to be the spectator and interpreter of God (1.6); he is the son of God (1.9); his duty is to attach himself to God (4.1), and like a soldier to obey God's signals and com-mands. He is to look up to God and to say: 'Use me henceforth for what thou wilt. I am of thy mind; I am thine' (2.16).

As Samuel Angus has pointed out in *The Mystery Religions and Christianity*, there is in Greek thought a strong strand which insists on the essential connection between God and man. 'We are indeed his offspring,' said Aratus, the Stoic poet, a saying which Paul was to quote (Acts 17.28). Cicero says that man is a god because he has the same control over his body as God has over the universe,[2] and that knowledge of the gods leaves us 'in no way inferior to the celestials, except in immortality'.[3] And this is a line of thought which the Christian writers repeat. 'The Logos,' said Clement of Alexandria, 'became man that from man you might learn how man may become God.'[4] Lactantius believes that the chaste man, who has trampled all earthly things underfoot, will become 'identical in all respects with God' (*con-similis Deo*).[5] 'Every believer,' says Methodius, 'must through

---

[1] *Letters* 41.1.
[2] *Republic* 6.24.
[3] *Nature of the Gods* 2.61.
[4] *Protrepticus* 1.8.4.
[5] *Divine Institutes* 6.23.

participation in Christ be born a Christ.'[5] And Athanasius says, 'He was made man that we might be made God.'[6]

On every side we meet the paradox of manhood, the fact that man is a helpless sinner, and the fact that man is somehow kin to God.

That paradox of manhood appears in all its sharpness in the teaching of Jesus and in his view of man. No teacher had ever a higher view of man than Jesus had. That is proved by his entire method of approach. No one ever flung such commands at men; no one ever launched such challenges at men; no one ever confronted men with such invitations. We have only to remember how much of Jesus' teaching and speaking consists of *imperatives,* culminating in the great imperative: 'You must be perfect, as your heavenly Father is perfect' (Matt. 5.48). There is no point in issuing commands, challenges and invitations, if there is no possibility of response. Jesus expected a response from men, for he worked on the assumption that every man has a sleeping hero in his soul. Jesus believed that man could make a response, even if it required his own death to make that response possible.

But this is not to say that Jesus thought lightly of sin. He did not see man through a golden and sentimental haze. The very fact that Jesus came into the world to live and die is the proof of the desperate case of man, entangled in his sin. As G. K. Chesterton once said, whatever else man is, he is not what he was meant to be. To Jesus, what mattered most was not the actualities of manhood but the potentialities of manhood. The important thing to him was not so much what man was, but what he could make him.

Bernard Falk, the famous editor, writes of the secret of the success of Lord Northcliffe. The secret was: 'He was never satisfied.' Today's results were only a foretaste of tomorrow's. 'You began your career with him every day. It was not what you had done that interested him, but what you were going to do.' Jesus was open-eyed to the sin of man, but at the same time Jesus believed in man with complete confidence, provided that man would accept the offer that he was making. The

[5] *Symposium* 8.8.
[6] *On the Incarnation* 54.

problem of manhood is sin; and, as Jesus saw it, sin operates within three spheres.

(i) There is sin *as it affects ourselves*. To Jesus sin is the failure to be what we can be and what we ought to be. The commonest word for sin in the New Testament is *hamartia*. *Hamartia* was not originally an ethical word; it was a shooting word; and it means 'a missing of the target'. Sin is the missing of the target at which life must aim, and which life ought to hit.

It is the man who failed to use his talent who is unsparingly condemned (Matt. 25.14-30). It is the salt which has ceased to be of any use as salt that is fit for nothing but to be cast out and trampled under foot (Matt. 5.13). It is the fig-tree which, in spite of every advantage, stubbornly refuses to bear any crop, which is in danger of complete destruction (Luke 13.6-9). It is the tree which does not bring forth good fruit which is to be cut down and cast into the fire (Matt. 7.18f.).

It is not suggested that men are equal in ability and that they can be equal in achievement; to differing servants differing talents are given (Matt. 25.14-30). But in one thing men can be equal—they can be equal in effort, for no man can give to life more than he has to give. Men are judged by how they use, and what they make of, that which they have; and a first law of the Christian life is that *uselessness invites disaster*. Sin is the determination to play selfishly safe, to preserve and to husband life (Matt. 16.24-26), and therefore the failure to be what we can be. Dick Sheppard conceived of judgment in terms of a man facing God, and God saying quietly: 'Well, what did you make of it?'; and that is indeed at least one of the standards by which a man will be judged.

(ii) There is sin *as it affects others*. Sin is failure in personal relationships in life.

(a) Sin is failure to respond to and to react to human need. That is the great lesson of the parable of the sheep and the goats (Matt. 25.31-46), and the parable of the good Samaritan (Luke 10.25-37). To see some one in need and to remain unmoved, or to pass by on the other side, or to be so unaware of others as not even to see their need, is sin. The human relationship should be a relationship of continual awareness issuing in continual help, and to fail in that responsibility is sin.

(*b*) Sin is failure in pity. The unforgiving servant, who had received pity from his master, had no pity for the fellow-servant who was indebted to him, and he was therefore condemned (Matt. 18.21-35). In the parable of the prodigal son the elder brother is implicitly condemned, and the reason for his condemnation is his lack of pity for the brother who had gone wrong (Luke 15.25-32). In the parable of Dives and Lazarus, Dives is sternly condemned, and the severity of the condemnation upon him is at least in part due to his callous acceptance of Lazarus as a part of the inevitable landscape of life, and his failure to see him as a person to be pitied and helped (Luke 16.19-31). As it has been well said, it was not what Dives *did* do that got him into gaol, it was what he *did not* do that got him into hell. Sin is the failure to reproduce in human life the divine pity of God.

(*c*) Sin is failure in respect for men. In the parable of the Pharisee and the tax-gatherer (Luke 18.9-14) the sin of the Pharisee was that he was completely certain of his own righteousness and arrogantly contemptuous of others. He was equally certain of his own goodness and of others' badness. To Jesus, contempt for a fellow-man is one of the most serious sins, and to be conscious of no sin is the greatest sin of all.

(*d*) Sin is failure in fellowship with men. It is separation where there should be togetherness. And the seriousness of such failure in fellowship with men is that it causes a breach not only between man and man, but also between man and God. No man can be at peace with God when he is not at peace with men. It is Jesus' instruction that, if a man is bringing a gift to the altar, and if he remembers, as he is bringing it, that there is an unhealed breach between himself and a fellow-man, he must leave the gift, go away and mend the breach, and only then come back and offer the gift, for only then will it be acceptable to God (Matt. 5.23f.). A man must be in fellowship with men before he can find the fellowship of God.

(*e*) To put it at its widest, sin is failure in love. The great characteristic of God is an undefeatable goodwill and an unconquerable benevolence to all men, good and bad alike. He makes his sun to rise on the evil and the good, and sends his rain on the just and the unjust. It is that undefeatable love that those who seek to be the children of God must reproduce in their lives

(Matt. 5.43-48). To fail to do so is to fall short of the perfection God requires, and so is to sin. Sin is the absence of love.

In our thinking about sin in regard to others, we have so far been thinking of it in terms of failure, that is, in negative terms. But there is a positive aspect of sin in regard to others. Of no sin does Jesus speak with greater severity than the sin of being the cause of sin to others. Jesus most sternly condemns those who put a stumbling-block in the way of others. The word which is used for stumbling-block is a vivid word; it is the word *skandalon*. Originally *skandalon* meant the bait-stick in a trap, the trigger on which the animal stepped, and which snapped shut the jaws of the trap. Later it came to have two general meanings. It meant anything which is calculated to make a man trip up, like a stone set in his way, or a rope stretched across his path. It meant a pit, cunningly dug, and covered over with the merest skin of soil or branches, so that, when the unwary victim stepped on it, it collapsed and engulfed him. Jesus says that any fate is better than the fate of the man who has caused another to stumble and fall (Matt. 18.6,7). When Robert Burns was a young man, he went to Irvine to learn flax-dressing. There he fell in with a man who introduced him to that way of life which was to be his ruin. In the after days Burns said of him: 'His friendship did me a mischief.' That is one of the most terrible of verdicts. It is sin to ruin one's own life; it is doubly sin to ruin the life of another. It is a terrible thing *to learn* to sin; it is a tragic and disastrous thing *to teach* to sin.

(iii)   There is sin *as it affects God*. The truth is that *all* sin affects God; *all* sin is sin against God. The Psalmist lamented: 'Against thee, thee only, have I sinned' (Ps. 51.4). To Jesus, also, that is the only true confession of sin.

(a)   Sin is taking our way of things instead of God's way of things, and doing so deliberately. Herein is the very essence of the temptations of Jesus (Matt. 4.1-11; Luke 4.1-13). Jesus was confronted with a choice between two ways of attempting to carry out his mission to men. There was the human way of bribing men with gifts, dazzling them with wonders, striking a working compromise with the standards of the world, a way which might well have led to a spectacular, if impermanent, triumph. There was the way of sacrificial love and loyalty and service, the way of God, the way whose inevitable end was the agony of the Cross. Which way was he to take? The way of human impulse, or the way of divine command? The condemnation of the scribes and Pharisees is that they set their own human traditions above the commandments of God (Matt. 15.1-9). The tragedy at the heart of the story of the prodigal son is that the son thought that he knew better than the father; his one desire was to get away from home, to take life into his own hands, to be independent, to do what he wished. Sin is doing what we like instead of doing what God likes. Sin is allowing our will to take the place of God's will. Sin is the deliberate denial of the basic fact in life that God gave us wills that we might make them his, and that in doing his will is our peace.

(b) Sin is the setting of self in the middle of the picture. It is living life in the conviction that we are the most important people in the world. Jesus drew the picture of the man who gives alms, the man who fasts, the man who prays, with the object of being seen by men. His aim is to focus the eyes of men upon himself (Matt. 6.1-18). Jesus drew the picture of the scribes and Pharisees, who wore dress which was ostentatiously pious, who loved the chief seats at any function, who revelled in the flattery and the adulation of men (Matt. 23.1-12). Sin is the attempt, either deliberate or unconscious, to occupy the centre of the stage. It is walking looking unto ourselves, instead of looking unto Jesus. Sin is the enthronement of self on the throne which God alone ought to occupy.

(c) There is another way to put this. Since God is love, all sin is sin, not so much against law, as it is against love. Sin is not so much a breaking of God's law as it is a breaking of God's heart. Therefore, sin is the deliberate refusal of the invitation of God. In the parable of the great feast, the condemnation of the guests is that they preferred going about their own business to accepting the invitation of the king (Matt. 22.1-10; Luke 14.16-24). In the parable of the wise and the foolish builder, the wise builder is the man who erects life on the foundation which Jesus Christ offers; the foolish builder is the man who rejects the offer and the way of Jesus Christ (Matt. 7.24-29). The condemnation of Capernaum and Chorazin and Bethsaida is that they had seen the mighty works of Jesus, they had seen God in action in Jesus, and had rejected him (Matt. 11.20-24). The condemnation of the generation of the Jews to whom Jesus preached is that they saw the wisdom of God full displayed in Jesus, and rejected it (Matt. 12.41f.).

Browning optimistically claimed: 'We needs must love the highest when we see it.' But the tragedy of the human situation rests in the very fact that that is not true. Men can see the highest and refuse it. They can be confronted with God's loving invitation, God's holy command, God's perfect truth, and they can deliberately refuse the invitation, reject the command, and remain blind to the truth—and therein is sin.

(d)   This is the line of thought which brings us to the consideration of the most terrible of all sins, the sin against the Holy Spirit, the sin for which there is no forgiveness (Matt. 12.22-32; Mark 3.22-30; Luke 12.10). For the correct understanding of the meaning of this sin two initial things have to be remembered.

First, we must note the occasion on which Jesus said this. Jesus had cured a demon-possessed man; the scribes and Pharisees had not denied the cure—they could not; but they had ascribed it to the fact that Jesus was in league with the prince of the devils. That is to say, these scribes and Pharisees could look on the Son of God and see in him the ally of Satan; they could look on incarnate goodness and call it incarnate evil. Somehow or other they had contrived to get their spiritual standards reversed and upside down.

Second, we must be quite clear that when Jesus spoke of the Holy Spirit, he must have been using the term in its Jewish and not in its full Christian sense. The only sense in which his hearers could understand the Holy Spirit was in the Jewish sense of the term. Pentecost and the full glory and promise of the Spirit had not yet come. What, then, was the Jewish idea of the Holy Spirit? According to Jewish thought the Holy Spirit had two supreme functions. First, he brought God's truth to men. Second, he enabled men to recognize that truth when they were confronted with it. The Holy Spirit, so to speak, operated from *outside* by bringing God's truth to men, and operated from *inside* by enabling men to recognize that truth when it was brought.

To this we must now add a further fact of life. If for long

enough a person refuses to use any faculty, in the end he will lose it. If a man does not use a physical skill, he will lose it. If a man refuses to use some accomplishment, he will lose it. If a man never uses some language of which once at school he had a smattering, he will forget even the little he knew. If a man reads nothing but trivial books, or listens to nothing but cheap music, in the end he will lose the ability to read good books or to listen to good music. If a man refuses to use any muscle in his body, it will in the end atrophy. When Darwin was a young man, he enjoyed reading poetry and listening to music, but, he tells us, he had so made his brain into a machine for recording biological data, that he never read poetry and never listened to music, and so he lost completely the power to appreciate them; and, he said, if he could start life over again, he would see to it that he kept the faculty of appreciation alive.

What is true of physical or aesthetic or intellectual faculties is also true of spiritual faculties. Let us, then, apply this rule here. If a man consistently enough and long enough refuses to accept and to listen to the guidance of the Holy Spirit, then in the end he will become quite unable to recognize that guidance when it comes. That is to say, he will be quite unable to recognize truth when he sees it. That is what had happened to these scribes and Pharisees. They had so long taken their way, they had so long refused God's way, they had so consistently rejected the guidance of the Spirit, that they had brought themselves into a condition that they were totally unable to recognize truth when they were confronted with it; they had come to a state when they could call good evil and evil good. That is the sin against the Holy Spirit, for it is the consequence of consistent and continuous refusal of the guidance of the Spirit.

But why should that be the sin for which there is no forgiveness? If a man has lost the power to recognize the good when he sees it, then he becomes unaware when he is doing wrong, and he becomes unable to feel the fascination of the good. He can neither feel remorse for sin nor desire for goodness. If that be so, *he cannot repent*. Penitence is an impossibility for the man who has lost the faculty to recognize the good. And without penitence there can be no forgiveness. Such a man has been shut out from forgiveness, not by God, but by himself. There, therefore, remains the truth, which, if it had been recognized, might have saved many from an agony of soul and even from the collapse of their reason—the one man who cannot have committed the sin against the Holy Spirit is the man who fears that he has; for, if he had, the days of the possibility of remorse would be past.

The essence of sin is to dethrone God and to enthrone self; the essence of sin is to take our way instead of God's way; and the dreadful consequence is that, if a man does that for long enough, he comes to a stage when he cannot recognize God's voice when he hears it, and when he cannot recognize God when he is confronted with him.

We have to still to see wherein Jesus' view of sin was new and original and far-reaching. To understand this we must first of all look at the three sins which Jesus most sternly condemned.

(i)   Jesus sternly condemned *self-righteousness*. In the parable of the Pharisee and the tax-gatherer, the tax-gatherer who sorrowfully confessed his sin and who in humility acknowledged his unworthiness went away a forgiven man, while the Pharisee who thought of nothing but his own merits went away unforgiven (Luke 18.9-14). In the story of the woman who was a sinner, who anointed Jesus' feet in the house of Simon the Pharisee, the contrast is between the woman and Simon; and the contrast lies in the fact that the woman was vividly, intensely, bitterly conscious of her sin and of her need for forgiveness, while Simon was not conscious that he had any need for forgiveness at all (Luke 7.36-50). As Jesus saw it, to be conscious of no sin is in itself sin, and specially so when the consciousness of virtue brought with it contempt for those whom it regarded as sinners.

(ii)   Jesus sternly condemned *externalism*. The Pharisees identified goodness with certain external acts, with the abstention from certain kinds of food, with elaborate and complicated rules of ritual washings, with a strict schedule and time-table of formal prayer, with the meticulous giving of tithes and the like. Jesus insisted that goodness has little to do with the physical condition of a man's hands but has everything to do with the spiritual condition of a man's heart (Mark 7.14-23). He likened the Pharisees to men who cleansed the outside of the cup but forgot about the inside; to whitewashed tombs which gleamed white on the outside but which were inwardly full of decayed dead bodies and bones (Matt. 23.25-28). To Jesus no external act, least of all conventional religious actions, constituted goodness.

(iii) The sin which Jesus most often condemned was the sin of *hypocrisy* (Matt. 6.2,5,16; 7.5; 15.7; 16.3; 22.18; 23.13,15,25-27; 24.51). Fine words without fine performance were anathema to him; it was by its fruits that a tree was known and by his deeds that a man was known (Matt. 7.19,20). It is not those who say 'Lord, Lord' who enter the kingdom, but those who do the will of God (Matt. 7.21).

The word 'hypocrite' is a revealing word. It is almost a transliteration of the Greek word *hupokritēs*, which means 'an actor'. A hypocrite is a man who acts a part, a man who presents the world with a version of himself which is in fact a lie, and it was precisely that sin that Jesus unsparingly condemned.

It is here that we come to the centre of Jesus' conception of sin. To Jesus sin is *an attitude of the heart*. It may be that a man's outward actions are beyond reproach, but that does not necessarily make him a good man; the deciding factor is the attitude of his heart.

The key passage is in Matt. 5.21-28. There Jesus takes two illustrations. The law says that we must not kill; Jesus says that we must not be angry with a brother man. The law says that we must not commit adultery; Jesus says that no forbidden desire must enter our hearts. Here was a moral and spiritual revolution. The ordinary view of sin was—and still is—that, if we abstain from certain forbidden deeds, we are good people. It is the teaching of Jesus that the thought and the desire are quite as important as the action and the deed. It is his teaching that we must not only not do the forbidden thing, but that *we must not even want to do it*. The test is not confined to a man's actions; the test includes the desires of a man's heart. This is new and revolutionary teaching, and immediately it lays down three great facts about sin.

(i) It brings all men under sin. We may well claim that we have never murdered anyone; we may well claim that we have never even struck anyone; but who can claim that he never experienced the emotion of anger, and who can claim that he never wished to strike anyone? We may well claim that we have never committed adultery; but who can claim that no forbidden desire has ever at any time entered his heart? It is Jesus' teaching that a man may abstain from these actions and from all such actions, and still be a sinner, if the desire to do them has been in his heart. The plain truth is that on many an occasion many a man has been kept from sinning by no higher motive than fear of the consequences. A. E. Housman wrote:

> More than I, if truth were told,
> Have stood and sweated hot and cold,
> And through their reins in ice and fire
> Fear contended with desire.

We may say: 'I am not a sinner, because I have not been guilty of any forbidden deed.' The question of Jesus is: 'Can you say that you have never *desired* to do any forbidden deed?' And that questions means that all men are sinners.

(ii)   This means—and it is a fact that runs all through Jesus' teaching—that the only person who can judge men is God, for God alone sees the secrets of the hearts of men. If we accept Jesus' teaching, it means that many a man confronts the world with an appearance of unimpeachable rectitude; he is full of good deeds; his attitude appears to be that of Christian charity and Christian forbearance; no one can mark in him an impure or an immoral deed. But beneath the surface, there smoulders a fire of concealed desire, of secret pride, of hidden bitterness, which God alone knows. A man can face the world with the face and even the conduct of a saint, while within him there is the heart of a devil. There can in any event be few men who would willingly allow anyone to see into the inner workings of their minds. In his book *The Meaning of Persons* Paul Tournier tells of the kind of thing which he is continually meeting in the course of his practice as a doctor. 'One man always acts with impeccable correctness, but only with great difficulty does he admit what his behaviour is like in secret. Another appears always extremely serious-minded, but has childish habits which he carefully hides. A devoutly religious man lays bare to me the intolerable tragedy of his life; he is generally thought of as an example of serene piety, whereas he is really haunted constantly by sexual obsessions.' Clearly God alone can judge this amazing complex of human nature.

Nor must it be forgotten that the other side of the matter is true. A man may appear to the world to be a constant and even a shameless sinner, and yet in his heart he may hate himself and his sin, and yearn for goodness. 'A man,' said H. G. Wells, 'may be a bad musician, and may yet be passionately in love with music.' God does not see only the evil desire; he sees the inward desire for that elusive goodness by which many and many a man is for ever haunted.

Only God can see the evil desires that are for ever kept on the leash, and only God can see the wistful yearnings which some-how never come to action; therefore, only God can judge.

(iii) If all this is true, it means that God is the only cure for sin. The plain truth of life is that a man may master his actions, but he can never by himself master his thoughts and his desires. The more he tries to do so, the worse his state be-comes. For that he needs some power outside and beyond him-self. In his autobiography, *The Living of these Days*, H. E. Fos-dick tells of his experience when as a young man he had a serious physical and nervous breakdown: 'I learned to pray, not because I had adequately argued out prayer's rationality, but because I desperately needed help from a Power greater than my own. I learned that God, much more than a theological proposition, is an immediately available Resource.' The only cure for sin, the only solution to the paradox of manhood, is the indwelling power of God. A man becomes a man, a man reaches his true manhood, when he can say with Paul: 'It is no longer I who live; but Christ who lives in me' (Gal. 2.20).

13

WHAT JESUS SAID ABOUT HIMSELF

BEFORE we begin to think about the teaching of Jesus about himself and about his work, it is necessary to start with a reminder. There is a tendency to think of Jesus' work entirely in terms of his death. But it must be remembered that the life of Jesus is every bit as important as the death of Jesus. It is quite clear that the death of Jesus would have had no value without the life which preceded it. To think of the work of Jesus without thinking about his life is just as serious an error as to think of the work of Jesus without thinking about his death. His work must be seen in terms of his life and his death.

There were three great descriptive titles by which Jesus was often addressed, and to which he would certainly have laid claim.

(i) Jesus regarded himself as a *preacher*. Early in his ministry he said to his disciples: 'Let us go on to the next towns that I may preach there also, for that is why I came out' (Mark 1.38). To preach was the primary object for which he came into the world.

The word which is used in Greek for 'to preach' is *kērussein*; this is the verb of the noun *kērux*, which means 'a herald'. The word *to preach* has in English come down in the world; it is a word which has acquired associations of dullness and conventionality without any thrill. But, when the word is used of Jesus, it means *a herald's proclamation*. It is a message from the King; it is the word of authority with no hesitations and apologies in it; it means that Jesus brought a proclamation and announcement from God to men. It is clear that Jesus regarded himself as having come to men with truth such as the world had never heard before. Jonah had been the most effective of preachers; Solomon had been the wisest of men, and had drawn visitors from distant places to listen to and to admire his wisdom; but with the coming of Jesus something greater than the supreme greatness of the past had arrived in the world (Matt. 12.41f.; Luke 11.31f.). Here was a message greater far than the greatest message of the past. It is significant to see how this word *kērus-sein* is used of Jesus.

(*a*) Sometimes the word is used absolutely (Matt. 11.1; Mark 1.38; Luke 4.44). The message of Jesus is *the divine proclamation of God to men*. It was not an airing of doubts, nor was it a weaving of fine-spun arguments. It had the accent of certainty and of authority, as of one who was not expressing his own opinions but bringing God's indisputable and unanswerable truth to men.

(*b*) Most often the proclamation is *the proclamation of the Kingdom* (Mark 1.14; Matt. 4.23; 9.35; Luke 8.1). We have seen that the Kingdom is a society upon earth in which God's will is as perfectly done as it is in heaven. The preaching of Jesus was the announcement of the will of God; the life of Jesus was the demonstration of life lived in obedience to the will of God; the summons of Jesus was the summons to accept the will of God; the offer of Jesus was the offer of power to live accord-ing to the will of God; the message of Jesus was that the time when the will of God would be supreme is on the way. The claim of Jesus was that he could bring to men the will of God, as no one else had ever done and as no one else could ever do.

(*c*) The proclamation is characteristically and essentially *the proclamation of a gospel*, the accouncement of good news (Matt. 4.23; 9.35; Luke 4.18). It was the news that the will of God is the salvation of men; it was the news of a God who was reaching out to men in love far more than he was pursuing them in wrath. It was the offer of the supreme gift of God to those who would receive it.

(*d*) The proclamation of the good news was not uncondito-nal, for it included *a demand for repentance* (Matt. 4.17; Mark 1.14f.). The offer of God is made to those who turn away from their past lives and who turn to him.

Jesus came to men as the herald of God's truth, God's will, God's love, God's demand upon men.

(ii) Jesus regarded himself as *a prophet*. In reference to him-self he said that it was only in his own country and among his own countrymen that a prophet had no honour (Matt. 13.57; Mark 6.4; Luke 4.24). When he set his face to go to Jerusalem, he went saying that it was unthinkable that a prophet should perish outside Jerusalem (Luke 13.33). The place of the prophet in God's scheme of things is expressed most essentially by Amos: 'Surely the Lord God does nothing, without revealing his secret to his servants the prophets' (Amos 3.7). The prophet is not simply, or even mainly, a *foreteller* of future events; the prophet is a man who is within the counsels of God, and who, therefore, is able to *forthtell* the will of God to men. Jesus came as one uniquely knowing the mind of God, uniquely in the confidence of God, so that he might bring God and the will of God to men.

(iii) Jesus regarded himself as a *teacher*. There are three closely inter-related words used of Jesus; in fact they all most probably go back to the same Aramaic word.

(*a*) There is the word *Rabbi*, to which the other two words go back. Six times Jesus is called Rabbi, five of them by his disciples and the sixth by a blind man appealing for his sight (Mark 9.5; 11.21; 14.45; Matt. 26.25; 26.49; Mark 10.51). *Rabbi* literally means 'My great one', and it was the title given by the Jews to the greatest and the wisest teachers. This was a title which Jesus was offered and which he accepted.

(*b*) There is the word *epistatēs*. Luke alone uses this word; Luke was a Gentile, and this is a characteristically Greek word, and Luke uses it as a Greek substitute for the Hebrew Rabbi. In Luke's Gospel it occurs six times, five times on the lips of the disciples, and once on the lips of a leper desiring to be healed (Luke 5.5; 8.24,45; 9.33,48; 17.3). This is a great Greek word. It is the word in Greek for a headmaster, and in particular for the man who was in charge of the *ephebi*, the cadets who were engaged in their years of national service of their country. The duty of the *epistatēs* was defined as being 'to lead the souls of the young men on the path which leads to virtue and to every manly feeling'. Here again Jesus is regarded, and regards himself, as the master teacher.

(*c*) There is the word *didaskalos*. *Didaskalos* is the normal Greek word for 'teacher' and in the Synoptic Gospels it is used of Jesus more than thirty times, as is the kindred verb *didaskein* which means 'to teach'. It is the word by which all kinds of people addressed Jesus. He is so addressed by his disciples (Mark 4.38; 10.35; 13.1); by the Pharisees (Matt. 9.11; Mark 12.14); by the Sadducees (Mark 12.19); by people who came to him with all kinds of request for help and for guidance (Mark 9.17; 10.17; Luke 8.49; 12.13).

The narrative of the Gospels shows Jesus teaching in all kinds of places and under all kinds of conditions; in the synagogues (Matt. 9.35; 13.54; Mark 1.21; 6.2; Luke 4.15,31; 5.17; 13.10); in the Temple (Mark 11.17; 12.35; 14.49); in the cities and villages (Matt. 11.1; Mark 6.6); by the seaside, with a fishing-boat for a pulpit (Mark 2.13; 4.1; Luke 5.3); in the streets (Luke 13.26), and in the inner circle of the disciples (Matt. 5.2; Mark 8.31; 9.31; Luke 11.1).

Jesus was the teacher *par excellence*, and it was the title by which towards the end he called himself. When he was making preparations for the last Passover meal, his instructions were to go to a certain house in the city and to say: 'The Teacher says, My time is at hand; I will keep the passover at your house with my disciples' (Matt. 26.18; Mark 14.14; Luke 22.11). It was as if he knew that that was the title by which he would be most easily recognized.

So, then, Jesus regarded himself as the preacher, the herald of God; the prophet, the one within the secret confidence of God; the teacher, the one who could bring men wisdom from heaven to meet the problems of earth.

We have even more direct information about the teaching of Jesus regarding his own work, for there is in the first three Gospels a series of sayings in which Jesus stated what he came to do.

(i)   He came to be *the Divine Physician of the sick souls of men*. After the call of Matthew, Matthew made a feast to which Jesus came. Matthew was a tax-gatherer, and his friends were in the eyes of the orthodox as disreputable as himself, and to the feast he invited these friends. At that feast Jesus also consented to be a guest. The orthodox religious leaders were shocked that any respectable man, and especially anyone who had any claims to be a teacher, should keep such company. How could any decent person be the fellow-guest of tax-gatherers and sinners? Jesus' answer was: 'Those who are well have no need of a physician, but those who are sick ... I came not to call the righteous, but sinners' (Matt. 9.9-13; Mark 2.14-17; Luke 5.27-32). Later Epicurus was to call his teaching 'the medicines of salvation', and Epictetus was to call his lecture-room 'the hospital for the sick soul'. When Antisthenes, the founder of the Cynic philosophy, was asked why he was so severe with his pupils, he answered: 'Physicians are exactly the same with their patients.'

Jesus regarded himself as the Divine Physician who had come to enable men to be healed of the universal human disease of sin. That is to say, Jesus did not regard the sinner with loathing and with repulsion. A lay person might find himself disgusted and revolted and sickened by some terrible physical condition; a doctor would find in the same condition only a call to his compassion and a summons to his skill. Jesus did not regard the sinner as a damned man; he regarded the sinner as a sick men. Jesus came, not to shrink away in fastidious horror from the disease of sin, not complacently to shut his eyes to sin and to pretend that it did not exist, not to palliate and to excuse sin; he came to be the Divine Physician who has the cure for sin. The very fact that Jesus could think of himself in this way is the proof that the desire of God is not for the destruction but for the healing of the sinner.

(ii) He came to be *the Divine Servant of men*. There was an occasion when James and John and their mother Salome came near to precipitating a crisis in the company of the disciples. They came with the request that, when Jesus entered into his Kingdom, they should sit in the chief places of honour, one on his right hand and one on his left. The only throne which Jesus offered them was the throne of martyrdom. Very naturally the other disciples were angry that James and John had sought to steal a march upon them and to earmark the principal place of honour for themselves. It seemed for a moment that personal ambition and personal resentment were on the verge of wrecking the unity of the apostolic company. It was then that Jesus spoke to them of the only true royalty, the royalty of service, and ended his words by saying of himself: 'The Son of Man came, not to be served, but to serve' (Matt. 20.20-28; Mark 10.35-45).

Here is the proof that Jesus came into this world not so much to receive things from men as to give things to men; he came not for his own sake, but for the sake of men; he came not to dominate like a conqueror but to serve like a servant. It was a commonplace of ancient religion that men should sacrifice to

God; but it was something completely new that God should sacrifice himself for men.

(iii)   He came to be *the Seeker of the lost*. When Jesus passed through Jericho on his last journey to Jerusalem, he made the startling proposal that he would stay in the house of Zacchaeus. Zacchaeus was the chief of the tax-gatherers, and such a proposal would shock all patriotic and orthodox Jews to the core of their being. But Jesus laid down the principle on which he was acting: 'The Son of Man came to seek and to save the lost' (Luke 19.10).

It is essential to give to the word 'lost' its right meaning in a passage like this. It has not its theological sense of 'damned', condemned to destruction by God for ever and ever; it has its simple, human, sorrowful meaning of 'in the wrong place, going in the wrong direction, all astray'. Zacchaeus had set out on the wrong way to find real happiness and real success in life. In the journey of life he was lost—and there seemed no way back. Jesus came to find the men and women who were heading straight away from God, and who were, therefore, lost, and to turn them back to God, for the road to God is the only right road. He did not wish to annihilate sinners, he wished to find them.

There is here the closest possible connection with the idea of Jesus as the shepherd who seeks and finds the lost sheep (Luke 15.3-7). The Palestinian shepherds were expert trackers; they could follow the track of the sheep where no one else could even see a sign of it, until, often at the risk of their lives, and always at the expense of toil and weariness, they found the lost sheep and brought it back. Even so Jesus tracks down the sinner, the man who has taken the wrong road, the man who had got his life into the wrong place, the man who is lost, until he finds him, not to blast him with the divine wrath, but to bring him back within the circle of the divine love.

(iv)   He came to be *the Fulfiller of all that was best in the past*. 'Think not', he said, 'that I have come to abolish the law and the prophets; I have come not to abolish them, but to fulfil them' (Matt. 5.17). Here is Jesus' claim that in him there are fulfilled the highest hopes and dreams of the past. Before his coming men glimpsed the truth; in him they could gaze on the full vision of the truth. Before his coming men heard faint echoes of the voice of God; in him they heard clearly and unmistakably the voice of God. Before his coming they had their gropings towards that which life should be; in him they saw life and received life, and life more abundant. Before his coming men had a knowledge of God, of the will of God, and of goodness which was partial and fragmentary; in him there came to them the perfect knowledge of God and of God's will. In the old Joseph story there is a wistful text. Joseph in prison came upon the imprisoned servants of Pharaoh's household and they were troubled; and the reason of their trouble was in their own words: 'We have had dreams, and there is no one to interpret them' (Gen. 40.8). Jesus is the great interpreter and fulfiller of the dreams which haunt the minds and hearts of men.

(v)   He came to be *the Divine Liberator of mankind*. 'The Son of Man,' he said, 'came . . . to give his life as a ransom for many' (Mark 10.45). Men were in the power of sin, captured by sin as a brigand captures a traveller on a journey, in servitude to sin as a man is a slave to a master from whom he cannot escape, a slave who can never pay the price of his own freedom, and by the work of Jesus man is liberated from the evil power which has him in its grip and from the fetters of sin which bind him. Jesus is the emancipator of mankind from the power of sin.

(vi)   He came as *the Saviour of men*. There is one saying of Jesus which is entirely characteristic and peculiarly revealing. On the road to Jerusalem Jesus and his men came to a Samaritan village. They requested hospitality, and not surprisingly they were rebuffed. Thereupon James and John wished to call down fire from heaven and to obliterate the inhospitable village, but Jesus forbade it. 'The Son of Man,' he said, 'came not to destroy men's lives but to save them' (Luke 9.56). Therein is the very essence of the gospel. It was not for destruction but for salvation that Jesus came into the world. Even when men opposed him, his one desire was not to wipe them out, but even then to save them. His great aim was to save men both from the continued folly and the ultimate consequences of their sin.

Here then we have Jesus characterized in his own words—the Divine *Physician* come to cure men from the universal human disease of sin; the Divine *Servant* come to spend himself for others; the tireless *Seeker* searching for men who had got life into the wrong place, and who were travelling on the wrong road in the wrong direction; the great *Fulfiller* of all the hopes and dreams and visions which have lodged within the hearts of men; the Divine *Liberator* come to set men free from the grip and the power of sin; the *Saviour* of men who would not even destroy his enemies, but who sought to the end to save them from their folly and from all that their folly would bring in time and in eternity.

But there is another side to this picture, and without the other side the picture would be but half drawn. To leave the picture there would be to leave a picture in which there is nothing but gentleness, but there is iron in the picture too.

(i) Jesus came with the demand for *implicit obedience*. He told the story of the wise and the foolish builders, of how the one chose for his house a foundation so strong that no storm could shake the house, and of how the other chose for his house a foundation so infirm that the storms shattered it into ruin (Matt. 7.24-27). The implication of this story is quite clear. The claim of Jesus is that he and his teaching are the only possible foundation for life, that the man who founds his life on him is certain of safety and that the man who refuses to found his life on him is certain of disaster. There are few men in history who have dared to say that obedience to them is the only foundation for life.

(ii) He came with the claim for *complete loyalty*. The claim of Jesus for loyalty is explicit and unique. 'He who loves father or mother more than me is not worthy of me, and he who loves son or daughter more than me is not worthy of me' (Matt. 10.37). 'If anyone comes to me and does not hate his own father and mother and wife and children and brothers and sisters, yes, and even his own life, he cannot be my disciple' (Luke 14.26). This is to say that it is the demand of Jesus that loyalty to him must take precedence of even the supreme human loyalties of life. He came with the demand that he must be given a place in a man's life which not even his nearest and dearest can share.

(iii) He came as *the great disturber*. 'Do not think,' he said, 'that I have come to bring peace on earth; I have not come to bring peace, but a sword' (Matt. 10.34). It was the plain fact of history that when Christianity first came into this world it frequently split families into two. One of the earliest charges levelled against the Christians was that they tampered with domestic relations. Most people wish nothing more than to be left alone, and, when Jesus enters a man's life, he shakes him out of his comfortable lethargy. No man can invite Jesus into his life and remain the way he is. It is true that Jesus offers peace, but it is the peace which only comes after a battle which may tear a man's heart out.

(iv) He came as *the agent of judgment*. 'I came,' he said, 'to cast fire on the earth; and would that it were already kindled!' (Luke 12.49). Fire is always the symbol of judgment in biblical language. Fire is that which burns out the alloy and leaves the metal pure. Jesus came to bring the cleansing fire of God in judgment upon sin.

(v) He came as *the touchstone of God*. It was his claim—and no claim can go any further—that a man's reaction to him settled that man's eternal destiny. 'Whoever is ashamed of me and of my words,' he said, 'of him will the Son of man be ashamed when he comes in his glory' (Luke 9.26; Mark 8.38). 'Everyone who acknowledges me before men, the Son of man also will acknowledge before the angels of God; but he who denies me before men will be denied before the angels of God' (Luke 12.8f.; Matt. 10.32f.). It is the claim of Jesus that response to him is the test which settles a man's eternal destiny.

So then Jesus came with the claim for absolute obedience, with the claim for complete loyalty, with the claim to have the right to disturb life, with the claim to be the agent of judgment, with the claim to be nothing less than the touchstone of God. If anyone makes a claim like that, he is either a deluded megalomaniac or the Son of God; he is either mad or divine. Which was Jesus?

14

THE SELF-CHOSEN TITLE OF JESUS

I F we place any reliance at all upon the Gospel records of the life of Jesus, we are compelled to conclude that *Son of Man* was Jesus' own most personal and most deliberately chosen title for himself. The title Son of Man occurs in the New Testament about eighty-two times, and with a single exception all the occurrences are in the Gospels. The one exception is the saying of Stephen in Acts 7.56: 'Behold, I see the heavens opened, and the Son of man standing at the right hand of God.' Within the Gospels themselves the phrase never occurs except on the lips of Jesus with one exception, and that one exception is a quotation of the words of Jesus. The question of the crowd to Jesus is: 'How can you say that the Son of man must be lifted up? Who is this Son of man?' (John 12.34). If we accept the account of the Gospels, this is clearly Jesus' own title for himself. Paul never uses it; the General Epistles never use it. To all intents and purposes no one uses it but Jesus; no one ever even addresses Jesus by that title. It is uniquely his title for himself, and therefore we are bound to try to find out what it means.

Jesus normally spoke Aramaic; in Aramaic 'Son of Man' is *bar nasha*; and that is the Aramaic phrase simply for 'a man', a member of the human race. If a rabbi was beginning a story or a parable, he would begin: 'There was a *bar nasha*, there was a man.' This is also true of the Hebrew of the Old Testament, in which the phrase would be *ben adam*, and would mean simply 'a man'. Again and again in the Old Testament the phrase 'son of man' means quite simply 'a human being', and appears as an expression strictly parallel to 'a man'. 'God is not a man that he should lie,' said Balaam, 'or a son of man that he should repent' (Num. 23.19). 'Blessed is the man who does this,' said the prophet, 'and the son of man who holds it fast' (Isa. 56.2). 'Put not your trust in princes,' says the Psalmist, 'in a son of man, in whom there is no help' (Ps. 146.3). 'What is man that thou art mindful of him, and the son of man that thou dost care for him?' (Ps. 8.4). The phrase 'son of man' normally means simply 'a man'.

To this we must add Ezekiel's characteristic use of the term 'son of man'. In Ezekiel the term 'son of man' occurs more than ninety times as God's address to the prophet. 'Son of man, stand upon your feet, and I will speak with you' (Ezek. 2.1). 'Son of man, eat what is offered to you; eat this scroll, and go, speak to the house of Israel' (Ezek. 3.1). 'Son of man, go, get you to the house of Israel, and speak with my words to them' (Ezek. 3.4). In Ezekiel the phrase 'son of man' contrasts the weakness and the frailty of Ezekiel's humanity with the knowledge, the strength, and the glory of God.

It is along these lines that certain interpreters of the Bible have sought to explain Jesus' use of the title. Such explanations have taken four lines.

(a)   It is suggested that when Jesus spoke as Son of Man he was speaking in terms of his human nature, and that when he spoke as Son of God he was speaking in terms of his divine nature. That view is in serious danger of turning Jesus into a split personality and of forgetting that in his one person the two natures were fused into one.

(b)   E. F. Scott in *The Kingdom and the Messiah* quotes two other explanations. It has been suggested that, when Jesus used the title Son of Man, he was thinking of himself in terms of The Man, The Representative Man, The Man in whom humanity finds its perfect expression, its perfect example, its consummation, and its peak. F. W. Robertson wrote of Jesus: 'There was in Jesus no national peculiarity or individual idiosyncrasy. He was not the Son of the Jew, or the Son of the Carpenter; nor the offspring of the modes of living and thinking of that particular century. He was The Son of Man.' That suggestion fails on two grounds. First, it is too abstract. Second, as we shall go on to see, it does not fit the facts, for it is with the title Son of Man that Jesus in fact makes, not his most human claims, but the claims that are most superhuman and divine.

(c)   E. A. Abbott thought that Jesus used this phrase against two backgrounds, against the background of Ezekiel and of Ps. 8. We have already seen that in Ezekiel 'son of man' expresses human weakness, frailty and ignorance. But what of Ps. 8? That psalm very uniquely combines the idea of man's humiliation and weakness and the idea of man's likeness to God.

'What is man that thou art mindful of him, and the son of man that thou dost care for him?' There speaks the frailty of man. 'Yet thou hast made him little less than God, and dost crown him with glory and honour. Thou hast given him dominion over the works of thy hands; thou hast put all things under his feet' (Ps. 8.4-6). There speaks the divine destiny of man. The Psalmist shows man's *present humiliation* and man's *infinite potentiality*. So Abbott believed that 'by his adoption of the expressive title Son of Man Jesus sought to intimate that he stood for the divine potentiality in human nature. He was the Man in whom God revealed himself, and whose victory would deliver all men from their bondage.'[1] The objection to that view is simply its complicated nature. If Jesus did use the title Son of Man in that way, it is almost impossible that anyone could have grasped his meaning when he spoke.

(d) It has been suggested that, when Jesus used this title, he was deliberately contrasting himself with the visions of a Messiah who was a supernatural, apocalyptic, wonder-working figure, that he was deliberately disowning all such ideas, and that he was speaking of himself as humble and simple, a complete antithesis of the popular ideas of the Messiah. The objection to that view is that, as we shall see, Son of Man was in fact a messianic title, and a messianic title of the most superhuman and supramundane kind. The one thing that the title Son of Man would never convey to a Jew was the idea of humility and simplicity.

Each of these interpretations has its truth and its beauty, but we shall clearly have to turn in some other direction to explain Jesus' choice and use of this title.

There is one other view at which we must look before we come fully to grips with what we believe to be the right interpretation of this title. It has been suggested that, when Jesus spoke of the Son of Man, he was not speaking of himself, but of some one to whom he was looking forward, and for whom he was preparing the way. When he sent out his twelve apostles, he said: 'You will not have gone through all the towns of Israel, before the Son of man comes' (Matt. 10.23). That could certainly be taken to mean that the Son of Man was some one whom

---

[1] *Notes on New Testament Criticism*, pp. 140 ff.

Jesus was expecting in the immediate future. When Jesus was speaking of the final destiny of men, as Luke reports it, he said: 'Everyone who acknowledges me before men, the Son of man will also acknowledge before the angels of God' (Luke 12.8). That again could be interpreted as differentiating between Jesus and the Son of Man. But the fact is that, if we had only these two passages to work on, we could argue that Jesus looked forward to the coming of the Son of Man as some one other than himself; but against these passages we have to set more than eighty passages in which it is clear that Jesus is speaking of himself. There are, indeed, differing versions of the same saying of Jesus, which make it certain that Jesus was speaking of himself when he spoke of the Son of Man. In Luke 6.22 we read: 'Blessed are you when men hate you, and when they exclude you and revile you, and cast out your name as evil, *on account of the Son of man*!' In Matt. 5.11 we read: 'Blessed are you when men revile you and persecute you and utter all kinds of evil against you falsely *on my account*.' It is clear that, in these two versions of this saying of Jesus, *on account of the Son of Man* and *on my account* mean the same thing. We may confidently disregard the suggestion that Jesus thought of the Son of Man as some one other than himself.

It will greatly help us to understand Jesus' use of the term Son of Man, if we understand the problem which faced him. Jesus' problem was the problem of communication; but in his case that which he desired to communicate was not so much a message in words as himself. It would, therefore, be of the greatest value to him, if he could find a compendious phrase which would be a summing up of himself, and which would enter into and lodge in men's minds. In his search for such a title he might do any of three things. He might invent a completely new title which had never been used before. That he did not do, because Son of Man is not a new title and certainly had been used before. Second, he might appropriate a title which existed, but which was colourless and vague, and fill it with a new content, and so use it for his own purposes. That again he did not do, for, as we shall see, there is no more vivid title in certain aspects of Jewish thought between the Old and New Testaments than the title Son of Man. Third, he might take a title which was known, and which painted a recognizable picture, and he might use it in a way so new, so unparallelled, so startling, that men would be shocked and jolted into attention. Nothing awakens interest like the completely new use and application of a well-known thing. We believe that this is what Jesus was doing, when he took the title Son of Man as his self-chosen title for himself. What, then, was the lineage of this title?

Without doubt the origin of the title Son of Man is to be found in the Book of Daniel. In Dan. 7 the seer has a vision of the great empires which have hitherto held world power and world dominion. He sees these empires in terms of wild beasts. They have been so savage, so cruel, so callous, so bestial that they cannot be typified in any other way. There is the lion with eagles' wings (v. 4), which stands for Babylon. There is the bear with three ribs in its mouth (v. 5), which stands for Assyria. There is the leopard with four wings and four heads (v. 6), which stands for Persia. There is the fourth nameless beast, with iron teeth, dreadful, terrible and exceedingly strong (v. 7), which probably stands for the all-conquering might of the empire of Alexander the Great. These are the powers which have hitherto held the world in thrall, and they are describable only in terms of monstrous beasts. But now their power is broken and their day is ended. So the writer goes on:

'I saw in the night visions,
and, behold, with the clouds of heaven there came one like a son of man,[1]
and he came to the Ancient of Days and was presented before him.
And to him was given dominion and glory and kingdom,
that all peoples, nations and languages should serve him;
his dominion is an everlasting dominion, which shall not pass away,
and his kingdom one that shall not be destroyed' (Dan. 7.13f.).

The power which is to receive the kingdom is further defined: 'But the saints of the Most High shall receive the kingdom, and possess the kingdom for ever, for ever and ever' (Dan. 7.18).

The point is that the new power which is to inherit the ever-

[1] So all the modern translations; the AV 'like the Son of man' is wrong.

lasting kingdom is gentle and humane; as the previous world empires could only be typified as savage beasts, so this empire of God can be typified as a son of man. Further, the power which is to inherit the kingdom is identified as the saints of the Most High, that is, the Chosen People, the nation of God, the people of Israel. The prophecy of Daniel is a prophecy of the exaltation of Israel and the coming of a world power which is gentle and humane as the preceding world powers were savage and bestial; and just as the previous powers were doomed to destruction this new power is destined to last for ever.

Even in their darkest days, even when they were a captive and subject nation, the Jews never lost the sense of being the Chosen People, and never lost the confidence that soon or late the kingdom would belong to them and to God. To that end they never ceased to expect the Messiah who was to be God's agent and instrument in the liberation of his people and the bringing in of his kingdom. It was only natural that they should nourish their hearts on passages of prophecy like the Daniel passage. The Daniel passage said that the kingdom would be given to one like unto a son of man. It was, therefore, a very natural step that the Messiah, the delivering one, should come to be known as the Son of Man. If there had been nothing but the Daniel passage, the idea of the Messiah Son of Man might well have developed into the picture of one who was gentle and humane and kind, and quite unlike the savage world rulers who had gone before; but perhaps about 70 BC there emerged a book which spoke much about that Son of Man, and which sharpened and intensified the picture. There are many passages in Enoch which describe that Son of Man, and in all of them the Son of Man is a divine, superhuman, pre-existent figure waiting beside the throne of God to be unleashed with victorious power against the enemies of God. He has been hidden and preserved in the presence of God from the beginning. Before the sun and the signs of the Zodiac were created, and before the stars of heaven were made, he was named before the Lord of Spirits. He will come from God, and when he comes it is true that he will be a staff whereon the righteous may lean and stay themselves, and a light to the Gentiles. But he will mightily destroy the enemies of God and of the people of God. He will put down the kings and the mighty from their seats, and the strong from their thrones; he will break the teeth of sinners; as for those who will not acknowledge him, darkness shall be their dwelling and worms shall be their bed. Terror and pain shall seize men when they see this Son of Man. They shall plead for mercy; their faces will be filled with darkness and shame; the sword shall abide before his face; as straw in fire God's enemies will burn before him, and as lead in the water they shall sink before the face of the righteous and no trace of them will ever again be found. He will sit in judgment, and his word will go forth and be strong (Enoch 46.2-6; 48.2-9; 62.5-9; 63.11; 69.26-29). So, then, in Enoch the Son of Man became a divine, superhuman, apocalyptic figure, ready to descend in victorious power from heaven, breathing out slaughter and destruction, exalting the righteous but smashing the enemies of God, and bringing in the end all things to judgment. This was the picture of the Son of Man which the Jews knew, and this was the picture that title would paint in their minds; and it was not unnaturally a popular picture in days of national misfortune and distress.

Now let us turn directly to Jesus' use of this title. We can distinguish various ways in which Jesus according to the Gospels used this title.

(i)   He used the title Son of Man as a substitute for 'I'. 'Foxes have holes,' he said, 'and birds of the air have nests; but the Son of man has nowhere to lay his head' (Luke 9.58; cp. Matt. 11.19; 16.13; Luke 6.22; 7.34).

(ii)   He specially used the title when he was making great claims or declarations. 'The Son of man came to seek and save the lost' (Luke 19.10). 'The Son of man came not to be served but to serve, and to give his life a ransom for many' (Matt. 20.28; Mark 10.45; cp. Luke 9.56; 11.30).

(iii)   He used it in connection with the Resurrection. After the experience on the Mount of Transfiguration, his instructions to his disciples were: 'Tell no one the vision, until the Son of man is raised from the dead' (Matt. 17.9; Mark 9.9).

(iv)   He used it in connection with the glory which was to come, and into which he would enter. 'Hereafter,' he said at his trial, 'you will see the Son of man seated at the right hand of Power, and coming on the clouds of heaven' (Matt. 26.64;

Mark 14.62; Luke 22.69; cp. Matt. 19.28; Matt. 24.30; Mark 13.26; Luke 21.27).

(v) He used it in connection with his coming again. 'There are some standing here who will not taste death before they see the Son of man coming in his kingdom' (Matt. 16.28). 'The Son of man is coming at an hour you do not expect' (Matt. 24.44; Luke 12.40; cp. Matt. 24.27,30,37,39; Luke 17.24,26,30; Luke 18.8).

(vi) He used it in connection with the coming judgment. 'The Son of man will send his angels, and they will gather out of his kingdom all causes of sin and all evildoers' (Matt. 13.41; 16.27; 25.31; Mark 8.38; Luke 9.26; 21.36).

We are not claiming that every Gospel word that we have cited is a verbatim report of the words of Jesus. The salient and significant fact is that the Gospel writers, when they wished to report or depict Jesus speaking about such subjects, naturally thought of him as using the term Son of Man. If we pause here, we see that there is nothing in these uses of the term Son of Man which does not fit into the picture which we have already found in Enoch. This was a way of speaking of the Son of Man which was perfectly intelligible to popular Jewish thought. The majestic glory, the stern judgment, the ultimate triumph could all have come straight from the picture in Enoch.

(vii) But *Jesus repeatedly used the term Son of Man in connection with his sufferings and his death.* 'The Son of man will be delivered to the chief priests and scribes, and they will condemn him to death, and deliver him to the Gentiles to be mocked and scourged and crucified, and he will be raised on the third day' (Matt. 20.18; Mark 10.33; Luke 9.44; 18.31f.). 'The Son of Man must suffer many things' (Mark 8.31; 9.12; Luke 9.22; cp. Matt. 17.12,22; 26.2,24,45; Mark 9.31; 14.41; Luke 22.22,37; 24.7).

Here is something completely new ; here is something which had never before been even remotely connected with the Son of Man; here is something which would leave the hearers of Jesus shocked and incredulous and wondering if they had heard aright. And here is something which explains a whole series of problems which are otherwise inexplicable.

(i) It explains the reaction of Peter at Caesarea Philippi. At

Caesarea Philippi the sequence of events was that Peter made his great discovery; Jesus thereupon went on to teach his disciples that he must go to Jerusalem to suffer and to die; and to this teaching the reaction of Peter was violent: 'God forbid, Lord! This shall never happen to you' (Matt. 16.21f.; Mark 8.31f.; Luke 9.22). Peter's reaction was more than the reaction of appalled and horrified love. It was due to the fact that he was totally incapable of effecting any connection between the idea of the Son of Man and the idea of suffering, let alone the idea of death. To him such a connection was a contradiction in terms, something which was incredible, incomprehensible and impossible.

(ii) It also explains the violence of the reaction of Jesus to Peter's outburst. 'Get behind me, Satan!' Jesus said. 'You are a hindrance to me; for you are not on the side of God, but of men' (Matt. 16.23; Mark 8.33). Jesus, too, knew the idea of the Son of Man in Enoch. In his temptations he had been faced with the temptation to become that kind of Son of Man; and in this moment at Caesarea Philippi Peter was facing Jesus again with that very same temptation which had faced him in the wilderness at the beginning of his ministry, a temptation which was now all the more acute with the Cross looming ahead.

(iii) It explains one of the most puzzling situations in the whole story of the Gospels. We have seen that Jesus repeatedly foretold his sufferings and his death. *Why then were the disciples so utterly unprepared for them?* Why was it that the Cross came to the disciples as such a devastating shock? The reason is quite simple. They regarded Jesus as the Son of Man, and to the end of the day they never succeeded in effecting any connection in their minds between the Son of Man and suffering. It is one of the habits of the human mind that it shuts itself to that which it does not wish to hear. By a curious kind of selective process it accepts what it wishes to accept and rejects what is either frightening, disturbing or incomprehensible to it. The connection of the Son of Man with suffering was so revolutionary, so contradictory of every received and accepted belief, that the minds of the disciples could not cope with it, and never assimilated it. Majesty, glory, judgment, triumph, they could understand, but not all the warnings of Jesus could penetrate minds shackled to conventional beliefs.

(iv) It explains the paramount importance of the Resurrection in the belief of the early Church, and especially in the belief of the Jewish section of the Church. It has been well said that the Resurrection was the 'star in the firmament' of the early Church. It was the Resurrection which vindicated Jesus as Son of Man. If his career had ended on a cross, it would have been impossible to see in him the consummation of the idea of the Son of Man; but the triumph of the Resurrection clothed Jesus with the ultimate victorious majesty which was necessary for the completing of the picture.

It remains to ask one question. When did Jesus import this new and startling connection with suffering into the idea of the Son of Man? It is a notable fact that apart from two instances in Mark 2 Jesus did not use the term Son of Man until after Caesarea Philippi; that is to say, this title belongs to the closing act of his ministry. It has been suggested that Jesus set out with the highest hopes of winning men, and that only bit by bit was he forced to the conclusion that he would be despised and rejected and would end on the cross. This would mean that Jesus, so to speak, began with the Enoch idea of the Son of Man and only modified it to include suffering under the compulsion of circumstances. We have already produced our evidence that this is not so in our discussion of the baptism of Jesus. At his baptism he heard the voice which told him that he was at one and the same time the Messianic King and the Suffering Servant. From the beginning he saw both the Cross and the glory.

Jesus took and used the term Son of Man, not because he wished to enact and fulfil it as men understood it; not because it was so colourless that he could insert any meaning he chose into it. He took it that he might use it in such a way that those who heard him might be shocked and startled into listening and thinking. Even then it required the events of the Cross and the Resurrection to interpret it to the dull minds of men. But by his use of it Jesus expressed his own certainty that as the Suffering Servant he must accept the Cross, and that as the Messianic King he must enter into glory.

15

THE MEN AGAINST JESUS

WHEN we read the Gospels, it is very difficult for us to understand the implacable hostility and the envenomed hatred which could not rest until they had driven Jesus to the Cross. We find it almost impossible to understand why anyone who lived a life of such love and service and kindness and sympathy should have incurred such savage opposition. The opposition was quick to arise. As early as the second chapter of Mark's Gospel we find the suspicion and the criticism of the scribes and Pharisees in action. We find the opposition to Jesus centred in three groups of people—the scribes and the Pharisees, who together form one group, the Sadducees, and the priests. Let us take these groups one by one, and let us try to see why they hated Jesus so much that they strained every nerve and were prepared to use any means to eliminate him.

(i) The opposition to Jesus is consistently connected with *the scribes and Pharisees* (Matt. 12.2,14; Mark 2.16; 3.6; Luke 6.2,7; 14.3). The scribes and Pharisees cannot be understood apart from the Jewish conception of the law. In Judaism the word law is used in three senses. First, it is used of the Ten Commandments, which are the law *par excellence*. Second, it is used of the Pentateuch, the Five Rolls, the first five books of the Bible, which are the law as contrasted with the prophets and the writings which constitute the rest of the Old Testament. Third, it is used of what is known as the scribal or the oral law. Clearly the third was the last to come into being, but in the eyes of the scribes and Pharisees it was the most important and the most binding of all.

To the Jew there was nothing in this world so sacred as the law. 'The law,' they said, 'is holy and has been given by God.' They believed that the law had been created two thousand years before the world had been created, and that it would last for ever after the world had come to an end. They said that Adam had been created on the day before the Sabbath in order that he might begin life with an act of the observance of the Sabbath law. They even went the length of saying that God himself studies the law. 'There are twelve hours in a day,' the saying ran, 'and during the first three the Holy One sits down and occupies himself with the law.' It was believed that every single syllable and letter of the law was holy and divine. It was believed that the law contained the whole will of God, fully and finally stated, that nothing could be added to it, or subtracted from it, and that there was no appeal against its ordinances and verdicts.

Here we come upon the whole principle upon which the scribes and Pharisees thought and lived. If the law is the complete will of God, it must contain everything that is necessary for the good life. But, when we go to the law, what we find is a series of great principles. For the scribes and Pharisees this was not enough. They desired to find a series of rules and regulations which would govern every action and every situation which could possibly arise in life. If the law is absolutely final and complete, then it must follow that anything necessary for the good life which is not *explicit* in it must be *implicit*. So, then, throughout the centuries the scribes made it their business and their life-work to deduce from the great moral principles of the law an unending series of rules and regulations to meet every possible individual action and situation in life. In the hands of the scribes the comparatively few supreme moral principles were turned into an infinity of petty rules and regulations.

This mass of rules and regulations is what is known as the scribal or the oral law, or the tradition of the elders (Mark 7.3; Matt. 15.2). And the day was to come when this mass of scribal regulations was regarded as even more sacred and binding than the actual word of Scripture itself, so that it could be said: 'It is more culpable to teach contrary to the precepts of the scribes than contrary to the law itself.'

For many centuries this mass of material was never committed to writing. It was lodged in the memories of the scribes, who were the experts in the law, and passed down by word of mouth from generation to generation of rabbis. Midway through the third Christian century a summary of all this scribal law was written down. The name of that summary is the *Mishnah*, which consists of 63 tractates on various sections of the oral law, and which in English makes a book of almost 800 pages. Not content with this, scribal scholarship embarked on the task of making commentaries on the tractates of the *Mishnah*. These commentaries are embodied in the *Talmuds*. There are two *Talmuds;* the *Jerusalem Talmud* runs to 12 printed volumes, and the *Babylonian Talmud* to 60 printed volumes. To put it in a summary way, the law of the Ten Commandments under scribal development had finished up as a library —for ever unfinished—of rules and regulations.

It is necessary to see this scribal method in action, because it was Jesus' head-on collision with this whole conception of religion which was the immediate cause of his crucifixion. We can see this process at work in the development of the Sabbath law. In the Old Testament itself the Sabbath law is very simple: 'Remember the sabbath day to keep it holy. Six days you shall labour and do all your work, but the seventh day is a sabbath to the Lord your God; in it you shall not do any work, you, or your son, or your daughter, your manservant, or your maidservant, or your cattle, or the sojourner who is within your gates; for in six days the Lord made heaven and earth, the sea, and all that is in them, and rested the seventh day; therefore the Lord blessed the sabbath day and hallowed it' (Ex. 20.8-11). Here there is laid down a great religious principle, conserving the rights of God and of man. But this was not enough for the scribes; this had to be worked out in hundreds and hundreds of rules and regulations about what could, and what could not, be done on the Sabbath day. In the *Mishnah* the regulations about the Sabbath run to 24 chapters, on one of which a certain famous rabbi spent two and a half years in detailed study. In the *Jerusalem Talmud* the section on the Sabbath runs to sixty-four and a half columns, and in the *Babylonian Talmud* it occupies a hundred and fifty-six double folio pages.

How, then, did the scribes proceed? The commandment says that there must be no work on the Sabbath. The scribe immediately asks: 'What is work?' Work is then defined under thirty-nine different heads which are called 'fathers of work'. One of the things which are forbidden is the carrying of a burden. Immediately the scribe asks: 'What is a burden?' So in the *Mishnah* there is definition after definition of what constitutes a burden—milk enough for a gulp, honey enough to put on a sore, oil enough to anoint the smallest member (which is further defined as the little toe of a child one day old), water enough to rub off an eye-plaster, leather enough to make an amulet, ink enough to write two letters of the alphabet, coarse sand enough to cover a plasterer's trowel, reed enough to make a pen, a pebble big enough to throw at a bird, anything which weighs as much as two dried figs. On and on go the reguations.

It was the scribes who worked out all these rules and regulations; it was the Pharisees who devoted their whole lives to the keeping of them. The word *Pharisee* means either 'interpreter', in the sense of skilled expert in the Law, or perhaps more likely 'separated one', in the sense of a man who has separated himself from all ordinary people and from all ordinary activities to concentrate on the keeping of these innumerable legal regulations. This is to the scribes and Pharisees was goodness; this, they believed, was what God desired. To keep these rules and regulations was to serve God.

Let us take another example. Certain ritual cleansings and washings were laid down. Before a man might eat, he must wash his hands in a certain way. He must take at least a quarter of a log of water, that is, a measure equal to one and a half eggshells of water. He must hold the hands with the finger-tips upwards and pour the water over them until it ran down to the wrists; he must then cleanse the palm of each hand with the fist of the other; he must then hold the hands with the finger-tips pointing downwards and pour water on them from the wrists downwards so that it ran off at the finger-tips. This was not a matter of hygiene; it was a matter of ritual; even if the hands were spotless, it must be done. To do it was to please God, to fail to do it was to sin.

It can easily be seen that the identification of true religion with this kind of thing has certain inevitable consequences. Religion became *legalism;* it became the meticulous keeping of a mass of rules and regulations. Religion became *externalism;* so long as a man went through the right actions and the right ritual he was a good man, no matter what his heart and thoughts were like, and no matter how hard and unsympathetic he might be towards his fellowmen. Religion could very easily become a matter of *pride*. A man might spend his whole life keeping these rules and regulations, which were obviously impossible for ordinary people, and might then thank God that he was not as other men are (Luke 18.9-14). There were never more than six thousand Pharisees; and it was inevitable that many of them were proud and arrogant and contemptuous of the common man. In fairness to the Pharisees it must be remembered that they were completely in earnest. To undertake this mass of rules and regulations must have been a tremendous task, yet in that law there was their delight; they loved the discipline of it; in it all they saw the service of God. Even if they were misguided in their whole method and outlook they were none the less fanatical in their desire to serve God. The scribes and Pharisees clashed with Jesus on three main grounds.

(*a*) It is quite clear that under this system religion became the affair of the expert. Only the scribes knew the immense ramifications of the oral law; only the Pharisees could keep them. Obviously all this put true religion out of reach of the ordinary working man. He could not engage in the ordinary working activities of the world and keep the law. To keep the law was in itself a whole-time occupation. Religion in its higher reaches became the preserve of the expert and of the professional.

Here was the first objection of the scribes and Pharisees to Jesus. He had never been to a rabbinic college; he was not a trained scribe and a professional rabbi; he was a mere layman, a carpenter from Nazareth. What possible right had he to set up as a teacher and to presume to talk to men about God and about life? 'How is it that this man has learning, when he has never studied?' (John 7.15). 'What is this? A new teaching!' (Mark 1.27). 'Is not this the carpenter's son? Do we not know his mother and his brother and his sisters? Where did this fellow get these things he is talking about?' (Matt. 13.54-58; Mark 6.1-5; Luke 4.22-24). These experts in religion were horrified, scandalized, insulted that this untrained Galilaean should invade their territory and should dare to teach. This was accentuated by the respect and adulation which these scribes and Pharisees claimed and received. The very name *Rabbi* means 'My Great One'. 'Let your esteem for your friend,' they said, 'border on your esteem for your teacher, and let your respect for your teacher border on your reverence for God.' They laid it down that the claims of a teacher went beyond the claims of a father—for instance, if it came to a choice between ransoming a father and a teacher from captivity, the teacher must be ransomed first—for a man's father only brought him into this life, while his teacher brought him into the life of the world to come.

Into this world of religious privilege, religious precedence, religious prestige there strode this young Galilaean with his revolutionary teaching—and the scribes and Pharisees were shocked and offended. What right had any common man to talk about God? The religious professionals have never granted to the common man the right to speak about God, and the religious professionals of Palestine were determined to silence Jesus of Nazareth.

(b) There was worse to come. From the point of view of the scribes and Pharisees evidence began to pile up that Jesus was himself a consistent and deliberate breaker of the law, that he consented to others breaking it, and that he even incited them to do so.

In the story of the Gospels there is a dramatic development in the idea of Jesus as a deliberate breaker of the Sabbath law. When he first healed a man on the Sabbath in the synagogue at Capernaum, there was astonishment and amazement (Mark 1.21-27). Such a thing could not be done in a corner and hidden away (Mark 1.28), and soon there developed a Pharisaic system of espionage in which the emissaries of the Pharisees deliberately followed Jesus to watch him and to accumulate more and more evidence that he was an inveterate and deliberate and blasphemous Sabbath-breaker. The matter began with the incident of the disciples plucking and eating the ears of corn as they passed through the cornfield on the Sabbath day (Matt. 12.1-8; Mark 2.23-28; Luke 6.1-5). There was no question as to the legality of the plucking itself; the law expressly laid it down that a man might pluck the ears of corn as he passed through a field, so long as he did not use a sickle (Deut. 23.25). But, when this was done on the Sabbath, it technically broke no fewer than four scribal Sabbath laws. To pluck the ears of corn was technically *to reap* on the Sabbath; to separate the husks from the grain was technically *to winnow*; to rub the grain between the palms of the hands was technically *to grind*; and the whole process was technicaly *to prepare food for use*. The simple act of the disciples was a fourfold breach of the oral law.

In the eyes of the scribes and the Pharisees the matter became rapidly worse. The plucking of the ears of corn might be regarded as a private matter; but Jesus began publicly to heal on the Sabbath day. The Jewish law on Sabbath healing was quite clear. To heal on the Sabbath day was to work on the Sabbath day, and was, therefore, forbidden. There were certain necessary exceptions. Medical attention was permissible when life was actually in danger, as, for instance, in the case of diseases of the nose, throat, eyes and ears. But, even in such cases it was lawful only to take steps to keep a man from becoming worse, and not to make him any better. The trouble might be arrested, but not cured. So, it was lawful to put a plain bandage on a wound, but not a medicated bandage; it was lawful to put plain cotton wool in the ear, but not medicated material. Unless life was in danger, the oral law definitely and distinctly forbade healing on the Sabbath day.

This was a law which Jesus knowingly and deliberately broke. When Jesus entered into the synagogue where the man with the withered hand was worshipping, the emissaries of the scribes and Pharisees were there deliberately to see if he would heal in order that they might have evidence on which to accuse him, and, when he did, they went out and laid their plans to destroy him (Matt. 12.10-14; Mark 3.1-6; Luke 6.6-11). Here was open declaration of war: the scribes and Pharisees were there to watch; and Jesus in their presence deliberately broke their law. Here was calculated defiance. Nor did Jesus stop there. He healed the bowed woman (Luke 13.11-17), the man with the dropsy (Luke 14.1-6), the man who was born blind (John 9), and all on the Sabbath day.

Jesus' point of view was quite simple. He believed that human need takes precedence of any ritual rule or regulation. It was quite true that the life of none of these people was in actual danger; as far as their lives were concerned the matter might well have waited until the next day; but it was Jesus' conviction that no human being must suffer for an hour longer than was necessary in order to keep a ritual law. He cited the example of David who in the extremity of hunger and of need had taken the shewbread which none but the priests might eat (Matt. 12.3f.; Mark 2.25f.; Luke 6.3f.). He cited the fact that the law permitted that an animal which had fallen into a pit might be helped on the Sabbath day. How much more must a human being, a child of God, be helped (Matt. 12.11f.; Luke 13.15; 14.5)?

Here was a head-on clash. The scribes and Pharisees saw religion in terms of obedience to rules and regulations, to rituals and to ceremonies; Jesus saw religion in terms of love to God and love to man. The scribes and Pharisees were perfectly sincere. To them Jesus was a law-breaker, a blasphemer, a bad man, an underminer of the very foundations of religion. It was absolutely necessary to destroy him before he did any more disatrous damage to Jewish religion. It is one of the supreme tragedies of the death of Jesus that he was hounded to his death by the most fanatically religious people of his day, by men who genuinely believed that they were serving God and protecting the rights of God by killing him.

(c) There was one final difference between Jesus and the scribes and Pharisees. To the scribes and Pharisees the attitude of Jesus to sinful men and women was shocking and incomprehensible. He well knew that they contemptuously called him the friend of tax-gatherers and sinners (Matt. 11.19; Luke 7.34). When Jesus went to be a guest at the feast that Matthew gave after his call, the Pharisees demanded of Jesus' disciples how their master could bear to eat with tax-gatherers and sinners (Matt. 9.10,11; Mark 2.15f.; Luke 5.29f.). 'This man,' complained the Pharisees, 'receives sinners and eats with them' (Luke 15.1). When Jesus invited himself to the house of Zacchaeus, the scandalized exclamation was: 'He has gone in to be the guest of a man who is a sinner' (Luke 19.7). Jesus believed that there is joy in heaven over one sinner who repents and comes home (Luke 15.7,10). The scribes and Pharisees said: 'There is joy before God when those who provoke him perish from the world.'

This attitude coloured the whole relationship of the Pharisees with their fellowmen. The Pharisees regarded ordinary people who did not keep the whole scribal law as unclean. Even to

touch the garment of such a person was to be defiled. A Pharisee
was forbidden to receive a non-Pharisee as a guest or to be the
guest of such a person; a Pharisee would never dream of entering
the house of such a person, of sitting at meat with such a person,
or of entering into even the remotest fellowship with such a
person. Their one aim was to have nothing whatever to do with
the sinner; the one aim of Jesus was to get alongside the sinner
and to woo him back to God.

Here was another head-on collision. The Pharisees narrowed
the love of God until it included only themselves; Jesus widened
the love of God until it reached out to all men, saints and sinners
alike. There can be no common ground between a religion
which sees the sinner as a man to be avoided at all costs and a
religion which sees the sinner as a man to be sought out at all
costs, between a religion which sees the sinner as man to be
saved and a religion which sees the sinner as a man to be destroyed. The inevitable conclusion of the Pharisaic mind was that
Jesus himself was like the company whom he sought out, and
that he was making light of, and even encouraging, sin. Once
again he seemed to them an evil moral influence, an undoer of
the work of God, a character so dangerous to true religion and
all that true religion stood for, that he must be immediately
eliminated before he could do any more harm.

There is the very stuff of tragedy in this situation. The Pharisees were the spiritual aristocracy of their age; no body of men
in history ever took their religion more seriously and in more
earnest. As Paul was later to say they had zeal, but not zeal
according to knowledge (Rom. 10.2). Because their religion was
a religion of legalism they could not understand a religion of
love; because Jesus was not one of the group of professional
religious experts, they believed that he had no right to speak at
all; because he did not keep the petty details of the scribal law,
they believed him to be a bad man; because he sought out sinners, they believed him to be a sinner. There was no possible
chance of agreement here. The Pharisees in their mistaken zeal
for God were determined to eliminate the Son of God.

(ii)   Into the opposition to Jesus there entered *the Sadducees*.
We often speak of the Pharisees and Sadducees together, as if

they jointly formed one group. But in point of fact the Pharisees and the Sadducees were very different, and their beliefs were well-nigh opposite to each other. The Pharisees believed in the resurrection of the body and in judgment to come; the Sadducees did not. On one occasion Paul used this point of difference to throw the Sanhedrin into complete confusion and to set the Pharisees and Sadducees arguing so violently with each other that they almost forgot him (Acts 23.6-10). The Pharisees believed in angels and spirits; the Sadducees did not. The Pharisees believed in the freedom of the will and in individual choice; the Sadducees did not.

But there was one basic difference between the Pharisees and the Sadducees. The scribal or oral law was to the Pharisees the greatest and the most sacred thing in the world. The Sadducees rejected the whole of it. They accepted only what was written in Scripture and would have nothing to do with the scribal elaborations of it; and of Scripture they only accepted the Pentateuch, the first five books of the Old Testament, and did not give any authoritative place either to the prophets or to the writings. 'The Sadducees,' says Josephus, 'say that only what is written is to be esteemed as legal. On the contrary, what has come down to us from the tradition of the fathers need not be observed.'[1] The Sadducees did not accept the mass of rules and regulations on which the Pharisees founded religion and life.

But the distinguishing characteristic of the Sadducees was that they were the aristocrats of the Jews. 'They only gain the well-to-do,' said Josephus, 'they have not the people on their side.' 'This doctrine has reached few individuals, but these are of the first consideration.'[2] Just because of this the Sadducees were the collaborators with Rome; they were well content to cooperate with their Roman masters in the government of Palestine. It is usually among the wealthy that political collaborators are found in any conquered country, because the wealthy have most to lose, and because they are prepared to collaborate in order to keep their comfort, their wealth and their privileges. Such collaboration necessitated frequent association and meetings with

[1] *Antiquities* 13.10.6.
[2] *Antiquities* 13.10.6; 18.1.4.

the Gentiles which for a Pharisee would have been impossible and unthinkable. The scribal law laid it down: 'Six things are laid down by the rabbis about the man who does not keep the law: 'entrust no testimony to him, take no testimony from him, trust him with no secret, do not appoint him the guardian of an orphan, do not make him the custodian of any charitable funds, do not accompany him upon a journey.' The strict Pharisee would never enter the house of a Gentile, or allow a Gentile to enter his. He would not even buy anything from, or sell anything to, a Gentile. For him even ordinary things like bread and milk were unclean, if they were sold, or had been handled, by a Gentile. For a Sadducee all this was quite impossible. The Sadducees would come into frequent contact with the Romans officials, would entertain them in their houses, and would be entertained in theirs. There were even Sadducees who were in sympathy with Greek culture and with the Greek way of life. To a Pharisee a Sadducee would be unclean, and nothing better shows the virulence of the hatred of the Pharisees for Jesus than the fact that they were prepared to enter into a confederacy with the Sadducees to work for the elimination of Jesus.

Why, then, were the Sadducees as eager as the Pharisees to compass the death of Jesus? The real reason for the hatred of the Sadducees lay in the fact that they completely misread Jesus. They looked on Jesus as a political revolutionary ready to raise a rebellion against Rome, or they were at least convinced that it was in such a rebellion that his teaching must end. Luke tells us the charge on which the Jews brought Jesus to Pilate. In their private trial of Jesus the Jewish charge against Jesus was a charge of blasphemy, the charge that he had claimed to be the Son of God (Matt. 26.65; Mark 14.64; Luke 22.71). But that was not the charge on which they brought him to Pilate. When they brought him to Pilate the charge was: 'We found this man perverting our nation, and forbidding us to give tribute to Caesar, and saying that he himself is Christ a king' (Luke 23.2). That was almost certainly a charge concocted by the Sadducees, for they knew that Pilate would never listen to a charge of blasphemy, which would have seemed to him a mere matter of Jewish religion, but that he was bound to listen to a charge of political insurrection. It is further to be noted that the Sadducees did not expect and did not await and pray for a Messiah. Why? The Sadducees knew that the one thing Rome would not tolerate was political unrest and disturbance. Any governing party which allowed any kind of rebellion to arise would receive short shrift from the Roman imperial government and would certainly be speedily evicted from office. The last thing the Sadducees desired was political trouble, for then they would lose their power, their prestige, their comfort, their wealth. It was all in their interests to keep things as they were. For them the coming of the Messiah would be, as they saw it, a disaster. Their thoughts ran like this: 'This man may at any moment put himself at the head of a revolution. Undoubtedly he has unique powers, and undoubtedly the people would follow him. Even if he does not himself do so, his teaching is so explosive that he may raise forces which will erupt even independently of him. If that happens, there will be trouble with the Romans. True, he himself will be crushed. But, if there is trouble, we will lose our jobs in the government and in the administration; our wealth will be confiscated, our place will be lost; our luxury and our comfort will be gone; and that must not happen.'

The hatred of the Sadducees was based entirely on self-interest. In Jesus they saw a threat to their privileges; therefore Jesus must go. The Pharisees hated Jesus because they were men of principle, however misguided their principles were. The Sadducees hated Jesus because they were the complete time-servers. The Pharisees hated Jesus from religious motives, even if these motives were entirely mistaken. The Sadducees hated Jesus for no other reason than worldly and materialistic selfishness. To ensure their own continued comfort and luxury the Sadducees were prepared to do anything to obliterate this perilous and disturbing Jesus of Nazareth.

(iii) There was a third group of people active in the steps which lead to the crucifixion of Jesus—*the priests*. Very often in the narrative of the Gospels they are described as *the chief priests*. The chief priests included two kinds of people.

(a) They were ex-High Priests. In the days of Israel's independence the High Priest was appointed for life. But under the Romans the high priesthood became a matter of plots, ambition and intrigues, and the High Priest became a pawn in the political game. It, therefore, happened that High Priests came and went rapidly, as one man after another plotted his way to the supreme office, or as the Roman government substituted one for another to suit its own purposes. Between 37 BC and AD 67 there were no fewer than twenty-eight High Priests. There were, therefore, always ex-High Priests alive; such a man was Annas; and these were included among the chief priests.

(b) Although the high priesthood was not hereditary, the High Priests were drawn from a limited number of aristocratic families. Of the twenty-eight High Priests we have mentioned, all but six came from four families, the families of Phabi, Boethos, Kamith and Annas. These families formed a priestly aristocracy, and their members were known as the chief priests.

At the beginning of Jesus' ministry we do not hear much about the priests, but that is because his early ministry was in Galilee and did not as yet impinge upon the priesthood, which was centralized in the Temple in Jerusalem. By the time of Peter's great discovery and confession at Caesarea Philippi, Jesus was well aware that the priests were his sworn enemies who would be in at the death (Matt. 16.21; 20.18; Mark 8.31; 10.33; Luke 9.22). When we come to the last days and hours of Jesus' life, as we read the narrative of the Gospels, we cannot help feeling that the whole scene is dominated from start to finish by the terrible malignity of the priests. It is true that the elders and the scribes appear on the scene, but the whole impression is that the driving force of the enmity to Jesus was the embittered, malevolent hatred of the priests. When Jesus spoke, they well understood his condemnation of them (Matt. 21.45). They were unhappy and displeased at the welcome Jesus received when he entered Jerusalem (Matt. 21.15). Very naturally they bitterly resented the cleansing of the Temple, and demanded to know what was Jesus' authority for speaking and acting as he did (Matt. 21.23; Mark 11.18,27f.; Luke 20.1). They are continuously shown as plotting to kill Jesus, and seeking a way to eliminate him without arousing the crowd (Matt. 26.3,4; 27.1; Mark 14.1; Luke 19.47; 20.19; 22.2). It was to them that Judas went with the offer of his treachery (Matt. 26.14; Mark 14.10; Luke 22.3f.). It was the priests who were behind the arrest in the Garden, and the Temple police were involved in it (Matt. 26.47; Mark 14.43; Luke 22.52). It was to the house of Caiaphas that Jesus was taken for the mockery of a trial (Matt. 26.57; Mark 14.53; Luke 22.54). The body which tried Jesus was meant to be the Sanhedrin, the supreme council of the Jews; that council contained scribes and Pharisees, Sadducees, elders and priests; but once again the impression is unavoidable that it was the implacable hostility of the priests which ruled the whole proceedings. They were prepared to hire false witnesses against him (Matt. 26.59; Mark 14.55). The High Priest was the principal cross-examiner of Jesus (Matt. 26.62-65; Mark 14.60-64). It was the priests who delivered Jesus to Pilate (Matt. 27.1,2; Mark 15.1). It was they who were the accusers of Jesus (Matt. 27.12; Mark 15.3; Luke 23.3-5,10). It was they who urged the mob to choose Barabbas and to refuse Jesus (Matt. 27.20; Mark 15.11), and they were the leaders of the shouts which demanded crucifixion for Jesus (Luke 23.23). They flung their mockery at him on the cross (Matt. 27.41; Mark 15.31). Even when he was, as they thought, dead, they could not leave him alone. They urged Pilate to set a special watch on the tomb (Matt. 27.62-66), and they tried to bribe away the evidence for the empty tomb (Matt. 28.11). In the last days and the last hours the leaders of that insane fury of hatred were the priests.

Why this enmity? To understand this we must understand the place which the priests held in Jewish religion. The only qualification for the priesthood was unbroken physical descent from Aaron. If a man possessed that descent, nothing could stop him being a priest; he did not possess that descent, nothing could make him a priest. Moral qualification and spiritual power did not enter into the matter. The only things which could debar a man from exercising the priestly function were certain physical defects (Lev. 21.16-23), of which the later oral law enumerated 142; but even if a man was debarred from exercising the Temple functions of a priest by physical defect, he was still entitled to the perquisites and the emoluments of a priest.

According to Josephus there were 100,000 priests. There were so many of them that they could not possibly serve all at the one time in the Temple. The whole priesthood was on duty only at the festivals of the Passover, Pentecost and Tabernacles.

They were divided into twenty-four courses, each of which served for two weeks in the year. This is to say that a priest's working year consisted of no more than five weeks.

The perquisites of the priests were enormous. Of all the sacrifices offered in the Temple, only the burnt-offering was entirely consumed by the fire of the altar. In every other case, only a quite small part of the victim was burned, and of the rest the priests received a very large part. In the case of the sin-offering, which was the offering not for an individual sin but for man as a sinner, only the fat was burned, and all the meat was the perquisite of the priests. It was the same in the case of the trespass-offering, which was the offering for particular sins. In the case of the peace-offering, which was the offering for special occasions of thanksgiving, the fat was burned on the altar; the worshipper received the greater part of the meat; but the priest received the breast and the right shoulder. The one remaining offering was the meat-offering, which was offered along with every other offering. The name is nowadays deceptive, for the meat offering consisted of flour and oil; it is called the 'cereal offering' in the Revised Standard Version. Of it only a small part was burned and the priests received all the rest. With the single exception of the burnt-offering there was no offering of which the priests did not receive a substantial part. No class of the people knew such luxury in food. In Palestine the ordinary working man was more than fortunate if he tasted meat once a week, whereas the priests suffered from an occupational disease consequent on eating too much meat. It is to be noted that even when a priest was not on actual Temple duty, and even if he was debarred from actually officiating at sacrifices because of physical blemish, he still received his full share of the offerings; for by far the greater amount of the meat which fell to the share of the priests need not be consumed in the Temple itself, but could be eaten in any clean place, and could, therefore, be distributed to the non-officiating priests in their own homes.

Nor did the privileges and perquisites of the priests end there. The priests received *the first fruits of the seven kinds* (Ex. 23.19), that is, of wheat, barley, the vine, the fig-tree, the pomegranate, the olive and honey. This offering was meant primarily as an offering to God, but its proceeds were enjoyed by the priests.

For the personal support of the priests there was brought to the Temple the *terumah,* which consisted of the choicest fruits of every growing thing (Num. 18.12). One-fiftieth of the crop was the average amount brought to the priests. In addition to this there were the *tithes* (Num. 18.20-22), which consisted of one tenth of everything which could be used as food. This was for the support of the Levites, but the priests received their share. Still further, there was the *challah,* or offering of kneaded dough. The priests were entitled to one twenty-fourth part of the dough used in any baking.

It can be seen that the priests were a privileged body of men in a comparatively poor country, living a life of unexampled ease and luxury at the expense of the people. It is not in human nature that men should willingly abandon a way of life like that.

Still further, the priests occupied a unique position between man and God. Since the time of Josiah all local shrines had been forbidden, and the law was that sacrifice could be offered only at the Temple in Jerusalem, and only through a priest. The priest, therefore, stood between man and God. If a man sinned, and the right relationship of God was to be restored, sacrifice must be made, and that sacrifice could be made only through the priest. Seldom can any body of men have wielded such spiritual power.

All this was true of the priests—and yet one thing was abundantly and increasingly clear—*if Jesus was right, the priests were wrong.* If Jesus' view of religion was correct, then the priesthood and all its functions were a vast irrelevancy. There are not lacking signs in the religious history of Israel that many times there was a breach between prophet and priest. Isaiah heard God say:

'What to me is the multitude of your sacrifices? . . .
Bring no more vain offerings;
incense is an abomination to me' (Isa. 1.11-15).

In face of all the paraphernalia of sacrifice Micah declared:

'He has showed you, O man, what is good;
and what does the Lord require of you but to do justice,

and to love kindness,
and to walk humbly with your God?'

God has no use for rivers of oil and thousands of rams; these are not the offerings he desires (Micah 6.1-8). Again and again the prophets with their ethical demands challenged the ritual of the priests. With Jesus the matter had come to a head. 'I will have mercy and not sacrifice,' he said, quoting Hosea (Matt. 9.13; 12.7; Hosea 6.6).

Here was the supreme challenge. Either Jesus had to go, or the whole sacrificial system had to go. Either the priesthood destroyed Jesus, or Jesus destroyed the priesthood. Beyond a doubt there were priests who loved the Temple service, and who through it sought devotedly to serve God; but, human nature being what it is, the vast majority of the priests must have seen in him a threat to their comfortable way of life, a menace to their spiritual supremacy, the assailant of their vested interests; and they decided that, before Jesus destroyed them, they must destroy him.

It was a queer tangle of human motives which hounded Jesus to the Cross. All the loveliness of his life mattered nothing. The Pharisees honestly and sincerely believed him to be a bad man and an evil influence on other men. The Sadducees wished only to remove a possible threat to their civil and political power and social standing. The priests were determined to eliminate a teacher whose teaching spelt the end of their perquisites and of their spiritual dictatorship. Jesus cut across blind and rigorous orthodoxy, political and social ambition, ritual and spiritual aristocracy; and so men came to the conclusion that he must die.

16

THE RECOGNITION OF JESUS BY MEN

JESUS was well aware of the opposition which was gathering against him, and of the atmosphere of hatred with which he was surrounded, and he knew that, humanly speaking, in the end his enemies would take his life away. He saw ahead, not the possibility, but the certainty of the Cross. This situation confronted Jesus with a question which demanded an answer. Was there anyone who had recognized him? Was there anyone who knew, however dimly and imperfectly, who and what he was? His Kingdom was a kingdom within the hearts of men, and, if there was no one who had enthroned him within his heart, then his Kingdom would have ended before it ever began. But if there was some one who had recognized him and who understood him, even if as yet inadequately, then his work was safe.

To this question Jesus had to find an answer. To find that answer he had for a brief time to disengage and disentangle himself and his little company from the tensions and threats which surrounded them, so that he could be alone with them. To that end he set out for the territory away to the north of Galilee to an area ruled not by Herod Antipas but by Philip the Tetrarch. On the road there was plenty of time for talk in which Jesus could open his heart and mind to the men into whose hands he must commit his work, when the arms of the Cross claimed him. So they came to Caesarea Philippi, and it was against the background of Caesarea Philippi that Jesus asked the most important of all questions and received the greatest of all answers. That background makes the question of Jesus and the answer of Peter all the more astonishing. There could have been few areas with more vivid associations than the area around Caesarea Philippi.

(i) In the ancient days the whole area had been intimately connected with the worship of Baal. It had been, as Sir George Adam Smith says in *The Historical Geography of the Holy Land*, one of the chief dwellings of the Baalim, and may well have been the Baal-gad of which Joshua speaks (Josh. 11.17; 12.7; 13.5). Thomson in *The Land and the Book* enumerates no fewer

than fourteen sites of ancient temples of Baal in the near neigh-
bourhood of Caesarea Philippi. Caesarea Philippi was a place
where the memory of the ancient gods of Canaan brooded over
the scene.

(ii)   In Caesarea Philippi the ancient gods of Greece also
had their dwelling place. On the hillside there was a grotto or
cave with a fountain of waters within it which was said to have
been the birthplace of Pan, the god of nature. To this day the
inscription 'To Pan and the Nymphs' can be traced in the stone
of the grotto. So closely associated was this place with the
worship of Pan that its ancient name was Panias, which still
survives in the name Banias which is the modern name for
the area. The hill, the grotto and the fountain of waters were
called Paneion, which means the shrine of Pan. Even to this day
the atmosphere of the old Greek gods broods over the place,
so that the modern traveller H. V. Morton speaks of 'the eerie
grotto'. Sir George Adam Smith describes the place: 'You come
to the edge of a deep gorge through which there roars a headlong
stream, half stifled by bush. An old Roman bridge takes you
over, and then through a tangle of trees, brushwood and fern you
break into sight of a high cliff of limestone, reddened by the
water that oozes over its face from the iron soil above. In the
cliff is a cavern . . . The place is a very sanctuary of waters, and
from time immemorial men have drawn near it to worship.
As you stand within the charm of it . . . you understand why the
early Semites adored the Baalim of the subterranean waters even
before they raised their gods to heaven, and thanked them for
the rain.' Around Caesarea Philippi there gathered the mystery
of the old Greek gods of nature, who were still revered and
worshipped when Jesus and his disciples came there.

(iii)   Still further, it was within this cavern that the River
Jordan was said to have its source and origin. Josephus describes
it: 'There is a very fine cave in a mountain, under which there
is a great cavity in the earth; and the cavern is abrupt, and
prodigiously deep, and full of still water. Over it hangs a vast
mountain, and under the cavern arise the springs of the River
Jordan.'[1] Much of the history of Israel centred round the Jordan

---

[1] *Antiquities* 15.10.3.

and the Jordan valley, and, therefore, Caesarea Philippi was compassed about with memories of the great things which God had done for his people Israel.

(iv)   But there was something even more impressive yet at Caesarea Philippi. In the time of Jesus Caesarea Philippi was one of the most beautiful cities in the East. In 20 BC Augustus had given it as a gift to Herod the Great; and Herod had built on the hill-top a great white temple of gleaming marble with the bust of Caesar in it for the worship of Caesar. 'Herod,' says Josephus in the passage which we have already quoted in part, 'adorned this place, which was already a very remarkable one, still further by the erection of this temple which he dedicated to Caesar.' In another place Josephus again describes the temple and the cave: 'When Caesar had further bestowed on Herod another country, he built there also a temple of white marble, hard by the fountains of Jordan. The place is called Paneion, where there is the top of a mountain which is raised to an immense height, and, at its side, beneath, or at its bottom a dark cave opens itself, within which there is a horrible precipice that descends abruptly to a vast depth. It contains a mighty quantity of water, which is immovable, and when anyone lets down anything to measure the depth of earth beneath the water, no length of cord is sufficient to reach it.' In due time Herod's son Philip inherited the area and the city. He further beautified the already lovely city and the temple, and he changed the name from Panias to Caesarea, 'the City of Caesar', and to the name Caesarea he added his own name Philippi, 'Philip's City of Caesar', to distinguish it from the other Caesarea in the south, which was the seat of the government of Judaea, and where Paul was imprisoned. So, then, at Caesarea all the majesty of imperial Rome and the worship of the Emperor looked down on Jesus and his men. Still later Herod Agrippa was to call Caesarea Philippi by the name Neroneas in honour of the Emperor Nero.

(v)   There remains one strange fact to add. It seems that Caesarea Philippi possessed the right of asylum; it was a place where the fugitive could find shelter and be safe. An inscription describes it as: 'August, sacred, with the rights of sanctuary, under Paneion.' In its history Caesarea Philippi must have sheltered many a fugitive, and it was there that Jesus went for shelter before the breaking of the gathering storm.

The history of Caesarea Philippi is written in the changes of its name. Originally it was Balinas, for it was the centre of the worship of Baal; then it became Panias, for men regarded it as the birthplace of the Greek god Pan; then it became Caesarea, because it was the city where Caesar was worshipped; later it was to become Neroneas, named in honour of Nero; today it has reverted to its ancient name, for it is called Banias, which is the Arabic form of Panias, since Arabic does not have the sound of the letter *p*.

It was here that Jesus asked his greatest question and flung down his greatest challenge, and surely there could be no more dramatic set of circumstances. Here was a wandering Galilaean preacher, who had begun as a carpenter in Nazareth and who had now no place to lay his head. With him there was a little company of men without education, without money and without prestige. At that very moment the orthodox religious authorities were resolved on his death as a dangerous heretic, and he was well on the way to being an outlaw for whom a cross was waiting. He stood in a place surrounded by the memories of the ancient gods of Canaan, a place where men worshipped the gods of Greece, a place around which the memories of the history of Israel gathered, a place where the eye could not miss the white splendour of the temple where men worshipped the majesty of imperial Rome; and there against the blackcloth of the world's religions, the world's history and the world's power, Jesus asked the question which demanded the answer that he was the Son of God. It sounds like preposterous madness. But the fact remains that the ancient gods are but a memory. Great Pan is dead. The Empire of Rome is dust. As H. V. Morton says, the great white marble stones of the imperial temple have become building material for the house of an Arab sheik. But Jesus Christ is still gloriously and triumphantly alive. The old faiths died; the old kingdoms fell; but the Kingdom of the homeless Galilaean still stands and still enlarges its borders throughout the world.

So, then, it was here that Jesus asked his all-important question. He began by asking what people were commonly saying about him, and the disciples told him that he was being identified with certain great figures.

Some said that he was *John the Baptizer* come back to life again. That was what Herod Antipas had already surmised (Matt. 14.2). John had made such an impact of greatness upon men that there were still those who felt that death could not have finally defeated him and could not hold him, and that in Jesus he had come again.

Some said that he was *Elijah*. This in its own way was high praise. To the Jewish mind Elijah had two distinctions. First, he was always regarded as supreme among the prophets. Even after the later great prophets had come Elijah was considered as supreme among the prophets as Moses was among the law-givers. Second, it was the Jewish belief, and it still is, that Elijah would return to earth to be the herald and fore-runner of the Messiah. 'Behold,' Malachi heard God say, 'I will send you Elijah before the great and terrible day of the Lord comes' (Mal. 4.5). If Jesus was to be expressed in human terms at all, he could not have been expressed in higher terms than in terms of Elijah.

Some said that he was *Jeremiah*. It was the belief that, before the Jewish people went into exile, Jeremiah had taken the ark of the covenant and the altar of incense out of the Temple, and had hidden them in a lonely and secret place on Mount Nebo, and that, before the coming of the Messiah, he would return and produce those treasures, and the glory of God would come back to his people (II Macc. 2.1-8). In one of the Old Testament apocryphal books God is represented as saying: 'For thy help I will send my servants Isaiah and Jeremiah' (II Esdras 2.18). Jeremiah was regarded as the foreruner of the Messiah and the champion of the people when they were in need.

Some said he was *one of the prophets*. Even if the people did not identify Jesus with a figure so great as Elijah or Jeremiah, at the very least they regarded him as a prophet, and, therefore, as a man within the confidence of God (Amos 3.7).

Then Jesus asked the crucial question. 'You,' he said, 'who do you say that I am?' And it was then that Peter made his great discovery and affirmed his faith that Jesus was none other than the Messiah and nothing less than the Son of God. The fact that Jesus did not accept the verdicts of the crowd, and that he pressed for a still deeper answer, tells us certain things about his conception of himself.

(i) It shows us that human terms, even the highest human terms, are inadequate to describe him. To call him Elijah or Jeremiah come back was great, but nevertheless it was not enough. 'I know men,' said Napoleon, 'and Jesus Christ is more than a man.'

(ii) It shows that to Jesus compliments are not enough. When men called Jesus John the Baptizer, or Elijah, or Jeremiah come back to life, they believed that they were paying him a compliment; they intended it as praise. To compliment Jesus and to praise him is not enough; nothing is enough except to worship and adore.

(iii) It shows that the only adequate way in which to think of Jesus is to think of him in terms of God. To say that Jesus is the Son of God is to say that there exists between him and God a relationship which is unique, a relationship which is such that it has never existed, and never will exist, between God and any other person.

(iv) It shows that all this must be a personal discovery. Jesus did not tell his disciples who he was; he encouraged, and even compelled, them to discover it for themselves. True knowledge of Jesus comes not from a text-book, and not even from another person, but from personal confrontation with him.

No sooner had Peter made his great discovery than Jesus made to him a great series of promises. These promises have been the subject of much and embittered controversy, and we must seek to find the mind of Jesus in them.

(i) There is the promise to Peter: 'You are Peter and on this rock I will build my church' (Matt. 16.18). Two things are to be noted. First, here there is a play on names, not reproducible in English. The Greek for 'Peter' is *petros*, and the Greek for rock is *petra*; in Greek there is a change in gender and therefore a change in the ending of the words; but in Aramaic the word play would be even more perfect, for Peter's Aramaic name was *Cephas*, and *cephas* is the word for 'a rock'. Second, whatever the meaning of this is, there is no doubt that it was a very great compliment to Peter. To call a man 'a rock' was high praise. A rabbinic saying says that God said of Abraham: 'Lo, I have discovered a rock on which to found the world.' Abraham, so the rabbis said, was the rock on which the nation was founded, and the rock from which the nation was hewn. The word 'rock', this time in Hebrew *sur*, is again and again applied to God in the Old Testament. 'Who is a rock, except our God?' (Ps. 18.31; II Sam. 22.32). 'The Lord is my rock, and my fortress, and my deliverer' (Ps. 18.2; II Sam. 22.2). There can be no higher tribute than to call a man a rock. To whom, then, or to what does the phrase 'this rock' refer in the saying of Jesus to Peter? Four main suggestions have been made. (*a*) Augustine suggested that the rock in question is Jesus himself, and that Jesus is saying that the Church is founded on him, and that Peter will be honoured in it. (*b*) It is suggested that the rock is Peter's faith, that, to change the metaphor, Peter's initial faith is the spark which kindled the flame and fire of faith which was ultimately to burn in the world-wide Church. (*c*) It is suggested that the rock is the truth that Jesus Christ is the Son of the living God, that this is the bedrock of truth on which the very existence of the Church is founded. (*d*) While we agree that there is truth in all these suggestions, we feel certain that the rock is none other than Peter himself. It is perfectly true that in the ultimate and eternal sense God is the rock on whom the Church is founded; but it is also true that Peter was the first man to discover and publicly to confess who Jesus was; and, therefore, Peter was the first member of the Church of Christ, and, therefore, on him the Church is founded. The meaning is not that the Church *depends* on Peter; the idea is, to use a modern metaphor from the same realm of thought, that Peter is the *founder member* of the Church, because he was the first to experience and to confess the Church's faith in Jesus.

It may be that we will get a better understanding of this saying of Jesus if we in fact avoid the word 'church'; in modern times it has the ideas of denomination, organization, administration, Protestant, Roman Catholic attached to it. It is true that in Greek the word is *ekklēsia*, but in the Greek Old Testament *ekklēsia* regularly translates the Hebrew word *qahal*, which is the word for the congregation, the assembly of the people of Israel, assembled before God and in his presence. The idea then is that Peter is the founder member of the new Israel, the new people of God, whom Jesus came to create, the company of men and women everywhere who confess that Jesus Christ is Lord. Nothing can take from Peter the honour of being the first stone in the edifice of the new people of God.

(ii)   It is then said by Jesus to Peter: 'I will give you the keys of the kingdom of heaven' (Matt. 16.19). The possession of keys always implies very special authority and power. The rabbis for instance had a saying that the keys of birth, and death, and the rain, and the resurrection from the dead belong to God and to God alone. In the New Testament the keys are specially connected with Jesus. It is the Risen Christ who has the keys of death and Hades (Rev. 1.18). It is Jesus who has the key of David and who opens and no man shuts, and shuts and no man opens (Rev. 3.7). These sayings all have a common background. They all go back to Isaiah's picture of the faithful Eliakim who had the key of the house of David on his shoulder, and who alone opened and shut (Isa. 22.22). Now Eliakim was the steward of the house of David; he was the doorkeeper who brought people into the presence of the king. So, then, Jesus is saying that Peter is to be *the steward of the Kingdom*. If that be so, *the whole emphasis is on the opening of the door,* for the steward is the person who answers and who opens the door. Peter was to be the man who opened the door of the Kingdom, and indeed he did. At Pentecost it was the preaching of Peter which opened the door to three thousand souls (Acts 2.41). It was Peter who adventurously opened the door of the Kingdom to the Gentile centurion Cornelius (Acts 10). It was Peter who at the Council of Jerusalem gave the decisive witness which flung open the door of the Church to the Gentiles at large (Acts 15.14).

The last thing that Jesus meant when he said that Peter would have the keys of the Kingdom was that Peter would have either the right or the duty to close the door; Jesus meant that in the days to come Peter would be like a faithful steward opening the door of the Kingdom to those who were seeking the King.

(iii)   It is then said by Jesus to Peter: 'Whatever you bind on earth shall be bound in heaven, and whatever you loose on earth shall be loosed in heaven' (Matt. 16.19). Here we must note two things. First, we must note that it is *whatever* you bind and loose, not *whomever* you bind or loose. This has clearly nothing to do with binding or loosing *people*. Second, the phrase *binding* and *loosing* was very common in Jewish language in regard to rabbinic and scribal decisions about the Law. To *bind* something was to *declare it forbidden;* to *loose* something was to *declare it allowed.* In this context this is the only meaning which these two words can have. Jesus was saying to Peter: 'Peter, in the days to come heavy responsibilities will be laid upon you. You, as leader of the Church, will have to take grave decisions. The guidance and the direction of the young Church is going to fall on you. Will you always remember that the decisions you will be called on to make will affect the lives and souls of men in time and in eternity?' Jesus was not giving Peter some special privilege; he was giving him a grave warning of the almost unbearable responsibility that was going to be laid upon him for the welfare of the Church in the days to come.

Jesus was saying to Peter, and saying with joy: 'Peter, you are the foundation stone of the new community which I came to found, for you are the first man to know me and to confess me. In the days to come you will be the steward of my Kingdom, opening the door to those who seek my presence. In the days to come you will have grave decisions to make, decisions which will affect men's souls. Always remember the duty laid upon you, and your responsibility to men and to me.' This is the natural and inevitable outcome of this whole incident. Jesus took his disciples apart for the all-important purpose of finding out if there was any who understood him. To his joy one man did understand, and Jesus was committing his work into the hands of that man, for that was the very thing he had set out to do.

But there is still something to add to this incident. No sooner had Peter made his great discovery and his great confession than Jesus began to tell his disciples of the suffering, the death, the Cross that lay ahead. And immediately Peter broke out with violence: 'God forbid, Lord! This shall never happen to you!' (Matt. 16.22). Peter's violence was due to two things. First, it is a desperate thing to hear the one you love more than anything else in the world saying that he is going to a cross. Here is the stuff of broken hearts. Second, Peter had just made the great discovery that Jesus was the Messiah, and *the one thing of which*

*the mind of Peter was totally incapable was to connect Messiah-
ship with suffering and death.* He had been taught and trained
from his earliest days to think of Messiahship in terms of victory, triumph, glory, conquest, power. A Suffering Messiah was
something which had never entered into his mind. Peter's heart
had gone out in devotion to Jesus, but Peter had still much to
learn, and Jesus had still much to teach.

And here is the explanation to two further things in this incident. First, this is the explanation of why Jesus instructed his
disciples to tell no man that he was the Christ (Matt. 16.20). At
that moment they were all still thinking in terms of a conquering,
fighting, nationalistic Messiah, and, if they had gone out to
proclaim Jesus as such, all that would have happened would have
been the tragedy of another disastrous and bloody and abortive
rising against Rome. They had made the discovery; as yet they
did not know what it meant; they must be silent until Jesus could
lead them further into the truth that suffering love can do what
conquering might can never do.

Second, this is the explanation of Jesus' violent rebuke of
Peter. 'Get behind me, Satan, you are a hindrance to me; for you
are not on the side of God, but of men' (Matt. 16.23). The truth
was that in that moment Peter confronted his Lord with the
very same temptation as that with which Satan had confronted
him in the wilderness. Jesus too knew the traditional idea of the
conquering Messiah; Jesus too had considered that way. No one
wishes to die on a cross in agony; but Jesus had deliberately put
aside the way of power, which he might well have taken, and
had chosen the way of the Cross. Peter in his mistaken love was
facing Jesus again with the temptation to take the wrong way,
and the temptation was this time all the stronger because it came
from the voice of love.

At Caesarea Philippi Jesus had the joy of knowing that his
work was safe because there was at least one who understood;
but at Caesarea Philippi Jesus knew that he still had the problem
of making those who loved him fully understand. But now the
way to the Cross was clear, because there was at least one human
heart in which he was enthroned.

17

THE RECOGNITION OF JESUS BY GOD

As the drama of the life of Jesus moved onwards towards the tragedy and the triumph of its close, there was a certain inevitability in the pattern of its events. It was inevitable that Caesarea Philippi should be followed by the Mount of Transfiguration. At Caesarea Philippi Jesus put himself to the test of *human recognition*; on the Mount of Transfiguration he put himself to the test of *divine approval*. It was essential that he should find out if there was some one who knew him and recognized him for what he was; but it was still more essential that he should be certain that the course on which he had embarked was in accordance with the will of God.

There were two reasons why Jesus had to be sure that the way he had deliberately chosen was the right way. First, the end of it was death, and, if the end of any course of action is death, a man must be very sure that it is the only way, before he sets out upon it. Second, the reaction of Peter must have sharply reminded Jesus once again that the course that he was following was a flat contradiction of all accepted Jewish messianic hopes and dreams and expectations. The popular expectation was of a day when every nation which would not serve Israel would utterly perish (Isa. 60.12); of a day when the labour of Egypt and the merchandise of Ethiopia, and the Sabaeans, men of stature, would come over to Israel in chains and fall down before her (Isa. 45.14; cp. Zech. 14.17f.). It was a career of conquest which popular thought marked out for the Messiah, not a career whose end was an agony on a cross.

Jesus called himself the Son of Man, and in the Book of Enoch, one of the most influential books between the Testaments, there was a vivid picture of a figure known as that Son of Man. That Son of Man in Enoch was a mighty and divine and supernatural captain, who had existed from all eternity, and who was waiting beside the throne of God for the day when he would be devastatingly and shatteringly unleashed upon the enemies of God. He would arouse the kings and the mighty from their thrones and kingdoms; he would loosen the reins of the strong, and grind to powder the teeth of sinners, he would put down the countenance of the strong and cover them with shame till darkness became their dwelling and worms their bed (Enoch 46.2-7). Before him the enemies of God would be as straw in the fire or lead in the water, and no trace of them would ever again be found (Enoch 48.9). With the word of his mouth he would slay all sinners, and the angels of punishment would be let loose to execute vengeance on them (Enoch 62.6-11). He would destroy the sinners and those who had led the world astray; he would bind them with chains in the assemblage-place of destruction, and the works of sinners would vanish before him from the face of the earth (Enoch 69.27f.). Here was the popular picture of the Son of Man, a figure of irresistible might and power who would blast his enemies from the face of the earth. There could not be a more complete antithesis to the conception that Jesus had of his work.

No wonder Jesus had to be sure. If he went on, he went on to death. If he went on in his way, he was the direct contradiction of all that men expected the Messiah to be. So Jesus sought God, for if God approved, the criticism and the opposition of men were as less than nothing. This is the essence of that event in the life of Jesus which we call the Transfiguration (Matt. 17.1-8; Mark 9.2-8; Luke 9.28-36).

Jesus took Peter and James and John and went up into a mountain to pray (Luke 9.28). Both Matthew and Mark call it a 'high' mountain (Matt. 17.1; Mark 9.2). One tradition identifies the mountain as Mount Tabor, but that is highly unlikely. Tabor is not a very high mountain, for it is not much more than a thousand feet in height. Further, on the top of Tabor there was a fortified city and an armed camp, the ruins of which still exist, which makes it a very unlikely place for the events of the Transfiguration. Still further, Tabor is south of Nazareth and a very considerable distance from Caesarea Philippi, and the Transfiguration took place within a week of the recognition at Caesarea Philippi (Matt. 17.1; Mark 9.2; Luke 9.28).

It is far more likely that the Transfiguration took place on Mount Hermon. Hermon is 9,400 feet above sea-level and 11,000 feet above the level of the Jordan valley. It is easy to climb; Tristram tells how he and his party rode almost to the top of it; but the climber can suffer from the rarefied atmosphere of the summit. Tristram says: 'We spent a great part of the day on the summit, but were before long painfully affected by the rarity of the atmosphere.' Hermon is no more than fourteen miles from Caesarea Philippi, and it was to Hermon and its slopes that Jesus went to meet God.

No one can ever know all that happened on Mount Hermon in this event, for the Gospel narratives are quite clearly attempts to put into words that which is beyond words. When we put the narratives together the story they tell is this. On the mountain top Jesus was transfigured until he became a figure glowing with light (Matt. 17.2; Mark 9.2f.; Luke 9.29). To him there appeared Moses and Elijah (Matt. 17.3; Mark 9.4; Luke 9.30). Matthew and Mark say only that Moses and Elijah talked with Jesus, but Luke says that they spoke with him about the departure which he was to accomplish at Jerusalem (Luke 9.31). It was Peter's instinctive reaction to seek to prolong this precious moment and to seek to remain withdrawn in the glory of the mountain top (Matt. 17.4; Mark 9.5; Luke 9.33). From Luke we gather that the events took pleace either late in the evening or during the night, for the disciples were overcome with sleep, and it was the next morning when they came down the mountain again (Luke 9.32,37). A cloud overshadowed and enveloped them (Matt. 17.5; Mark 9.7; Luke 9.34); and out of the cloud there came a voice, which was the voice of God, saying: 'This is my beloved Son, with whom I am well pleased,' and bidding them to listen to him (Matt. 17.5; Mark 9.7; Luke 9.35). The whole event is clad in mystery, and yet the meaning and the significance of it for Jesus are clear.

The significant feature of the Transfiguration story is the way in which its every detail either links Jesus with the greatness of the past or nerves him for the challenge of the future.

In Jewish story the mountain tops were always close to God. It was on Mount Sinai that Moses had received the Law from God (Ex. 31.18); and it was on Mount Horeb that Elijah had had his revelation of the God who was not in the wind, and not in the earthquake, but in the still small voice (I Kings 19.9-12). The very act of going up into Mount Hermon was the act of drawing near to God.

All the Gospels speak of the luminous cloud which enveloped Jesus and his disciples. A curious feature of Mount Hermon, on which travellers comment, is 'the extreme rapidity of the formation of cloud upon the summit. In a few moments a thick cap forms over the top of the mountain, and as quickly disperses, and entirely disappears.' The swift coming and going of the cloud were characteristic of Hermon. But there is more to it than that. All through the history of Israel we find the idea of the *shechinah*. The *shechinah* is the glory of God, and again and again this glory appeared to the people in the form of a cloud. In their journey in the wilderness the pillar of cloud led the people on their way (Ex. 13.21f.). At the end of the building of the Tabernacle there come the words: 'Then the cloud covered the tent of meeting, and the glory of the Lord filled the tabernacle. And Moses was not able to enter the tent of meeting because the cloud abode upon it, and the glory of the Lord filled the tabernacle' (Ex. 40.34f.). It had been in this cloud that God descended to give Moses the law (Ex. 34.5). Once again we find this strange mysterious luminous cloud at the dedication of Solomon's Temple. 'When the priests came out of the holy place, a cloud filled the house of the Lord, so that the priests could not stand to minister because of the cloud; for the glory of the Lord filled the house of the Lord' (I Kings 8.10f.; cp. II Chron. 5.13f.; 7.2). The cloud stands, as it always stood in Jewish thought, for the glory of God settling upon the place. The mountain top is the place of God, and on the Mount of Transfiguration the glory of God was there.

It was Moses and Elijah who appeared to Jesus. These were the two supreme figures of Jewish religion. Moses was the supreme law-giver, and Elijah was the supreme prophet. We have already seen how Jesus must have been very conscious of how his own conception of Messiahship was completely different from the popular conception; but here we see Moses and Elijah encouraging him to go on. It is as if they said to him: 'It is you who are right, and it is the popular teachers who are wrong; it is you in whom there is the fulfilment of all that the law says and all that the prophets foretold. The real fulfilment of the past is not in the popular idea of might and power, but in your way of sacrificial love.' The appearance of these two figures is the guarantee to Jesus that, however he might differ from the teachers of his day, he was none the less the real fulfilment of the message of God's great servants of the past.

But there is more than that. It is a strange thing that Moses and Elijah are the two great Old Testament figures about whose death there is mystery. The death of Moses on the top of Mount Nebo is a strange story. 'So Moses the servant of the Lord died there in the land of Moab according to the word of the Lord, and he buried him in the valley in the land of Moab opposite Beth-peor, but no man knows the place of his burial to this day' (Deut. 34.5f.).) It reads as if the hands of God himself laid his great servant to rest. There can be no burial scene like that in all history. The story of the death of Elijah is equally dramatic. Elijah and Elishah were talking together, 'and as they still went on and talked, behold, a chariot of fire and horses of fire separated the two of them. And Elijah went up by a whirlwind into heaven . . . and he saw him no more' (II Kings 2.11f.). Moses and Elijah both went out in glory. However much they had to suffer as the heralds and representatives of God, in the end, as the old stories had it, they seemed to be too great for death to touch in any ordinary way. They were the great representatives of those who witnessed and suffered for God, and for whom the end was not tragedy but triumph. Here for Jesus was the great encouragement that, if he went on, there would certainly be a cross, but there would equally certainly be the glory.

There is still something else in this event which at one and the same time linked Jesus with the past and sent him forward to the future. As Luke has it, Moses and Elijah spoke with him about the *departure* which he was to accomplish in Jerusalem (Luke 9.31). The Greek word here used for 'departure' is *exodos*, which is transliterated into English as 'exodus'. That word is for ever connected with one of the great adventures of history, the 'going out' of the children of Israel from the land of Egypt to set out on the journey across the desert in order to reach the promised land. They went out into the unknown with nothing but the command and the promise of God. In the very use of that word it was as if Moses and Elijah said to Jesus: 'Long centuries ago God's people set out upon their *exodus*, that great adventure of faith, which led them in obedience to God across the desert into the promised land. Now you, God's Son, are setting out on your great *exodus,* and it too will lead by way of the cross into the promised land.' The very use of that word *exodos* gave Jesus the certainty that, whatever the agony to come, at the end of it there lay the promised land.

But for Jesus none of these things was the supreme moment of the mountain top. Let us again remember what Jesus was seeking. He had to be very sure that the way which he was taking was the way which God wished him to take. It was for that assurance that he had come to Mount Hermon—and in that moment that assurance came to him. 'This is my beloved Son, with whom I am well pleased'—there spoke the voice of God's approval to Jesus, and the way ahead was clear.

One thing more this story has to say, and this one final thing throws a great illumination on the mind of Jesus. The whole Transfiguration story remains wrapped in mystery, but one thing is quite clear. In it there came to Jesus and to his disciples an experience of God that was unique. To that experience there were two reactions. The reaction of Peter was to take steps to remain as long as possible in the glory of the mountain top, to prepare three booths, and to linger there, and not to come down again (Matt. 17.4; Mark 9.5; Luke 9.33). The reaction of Jesus was to come down from the mountain, to rise, and to enter again into the engagement of life. When Jesus withdrew to pray, when Jesus went up to the mountain top, such action was never for him escape; it was always preparation. The experience of the glory of God did not prompt Jesus to remain withdrawn on the mountain top; it sent him out to walk with an even more certain tread the way that led to Calvary.

On the Mount of Transfiguration Jesus received the assurance that, however much he differed from the popular and orthodox view of the Messiah, it was his view which was the real fulfilment of all that the law and the prophets foretold. On the Mount of Transfiguration Jesus received the approval of God before he went on to his cross and his crown.